HOW TO PLANT
A TREE

HOW TO PLANT
A TREE

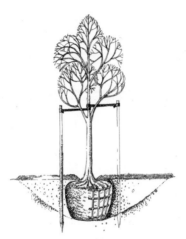

A Simple Celebration of
TREES & TREE-PLANTING CEREMONIES

~

DANIEL BUTLER

Jeremy P. Tarcher / Penguin
a member of Penguin Group (USA) Inc.
New York

JEREMY P. TARCHER/PENGUIN
Published by the Penguin Group
Penguin Group (USA) Inc.,
375 Hudson Street,
New York 10014, USA
Penguin Group (Canada)
90 Eglinton Avenue East, Suite 700,
Toronto ON M4P 2Y3, Canada
(a division of Pearson Penguin Canada Inc.)

Penguin Books Ltd
80 Strand, London,
WC2R 0RL, England

Penguin Ireland
25 St Stephen's Green,
Dublin 2, Ireland
(a division of Penguin Books Ltd)

Penguin Group (Australia)
250 Camberwell Road,
Camberwell,
Victoria 3124, Australia
(a division of Pearson Australia Group)

Penguin Books India Pvt Ltd
11 Community Centre,
Panchsheel Park,
New Delhi – 110 017, India

Penguin Group (NZ)
67 Apollo Drive, Rosedale,
North Shore 0632, New Zealand
(a division of Pearson New Zealand Ltd)

Penguin Books (South Africa) (Pty) Ltd
24 Sturdee Avenue, Rosebank,
Johannesburg 2196, South Africa

Penguin Books Ltd, Registered Offices:
80 Strand, London,
WC2R 0RL, England

This edition published by Penguin
Group (USA) Inc., 2010

Most Tarcher/Penguin books are
available at special discounts for bulk
purchase for sales promotions, premiums,
fund-raising, and educational needs. For
details, write to Penguin Group (USA)
Inc. Special Markets, 375 Hudson
Street, New York, NY 10014.

Library of Congress Cataloging-in-
Publication data is available on request

Printed in Malaysia
10 9 8 7 6 5 4 3 2 1

ISBN: 978-1-58542-796-3

This book was conceived, designed,
and produced by
Ivy Press
210 High Street, Lewes
East Sussex BN7 2NS, UK
www.ivy-group.co.uk

Creative Director: Peter Bridgewater
Publisher: Jason Hook
Editorial Director: Tom Kitch
Art Director: Wayne Blades
Senior Editor: Polita Anderson
Designer: Glyn Bridgewater
Illustrator: Andrew Farmer

CONTENTS

⟨⁓⟩

⟨⁓⟩

INTRODUCTION

*H*umans have always had a close affinity with trees. Long before our ancestors began to roam the African plains, let alone venture into a chilly Europe or across the icy Bering Straits into North America, Homo sapiens *were almost totally reliant on trees for almost all aspects of life. By day, the forest supplied food in the form of fruit, nuts, leaves, insects, honey, birds, and small animals. At night, the branches offered a refuge from predators. Travel writer Bruce Chatwin (1940–1989) believed this nocturnal escape to the canopy explains why babies are so easily lulled to sleep rocking in their mother's arms as her gentle shush echoes the wind in the leaves. Later, as the first hunter-gatherers dared to leave the safety of the woods, they still needed branches to make their hunting weapons, temporary shelters, and, of course, the fire that allowed them to broaden their diet and ward off nighttime predators.*

Trees were also essential as humans developed from hunter to farmer. Apples and figs were probably among the earliest cultivated crops, the first accidentally spread by nomads ranging over the Asian steppes. As the centuries passed, trees remained vital as a source of timber for increasingly elaborate buildings, tools, and boats.

Little wonder that over the millennia trees have become woven into the very fabric of every culture and religion. They feature in the myths and faiths of the world's oldest civilizations. Sacred groves and veteran trees were integral parts of the religions of pagan Europe and pre-Columbian North and South America. In the East, the banyan appears in Hinduism and Buddhism, while the Book of Genesis makes reference to the Tree of Knowledge.

Forest management

At first people simply cut down trees as they were needed, but as the primeval forests were cleared, the first signs of sylvan management crept in. The relatively low-value lime and birch scrub that covered much of Europe was increasingly replaced by more useful oak, ash, and beech. Large trees were given preference and selectively felled to provide building lumber, while smaller woodland species, such as hazel, were coppiced. At first planting was the result of natural regeneration, but over time foresters began to nurture seedlings and plant intensively to encourage straighter, knot-free lumber, not least to meet the demand for great wooden ships from European nations that sought to expand their empires through naval supremacy.

Then came the great classical gardeners of Europe whose landscaped grounds around palaces and stately homes relied on the visual impact of great and veteran trees. The next wave of interest in trees stemmed from the nineteenth- and early twentieth-century collectors who scoured the world for beautiful and remarkable specimens to grace botanical gardens and arboreta.

Arbor day

Trees played an important part in American history. Long before Europeans first arrived, trees were sacred to the native peoples, but after the seventeenth century, the commercial potential of the continent's vast forests was apparent to the newcomers. Pioneering nurserymen, such as Johnny Appleseed, have entered the folklore of the West, while in 1872 the Nebraskan J. Sterling Morton set up a national tree planting festival, Arbor Day, which was targeted particularly at schoolchildren. The idea was an immediate success. By 1885, it was declared a legal holiday in Nebraska and other states quickly followed suit. The original aim was principally to improve agriculture by providing shelter and preventing soil erosion on the Great Plains. Over time, Arbor Day has become an environmental and conservation movement. Today, National Arbor Day is celebrated on the last Friday in April, although some states celebrate it on a different day due to the local climate.

Environmentalism

In our own time, there is deep-rooted environmental concern about the impact of humans on the planet. First there were warning signs about the potentially tragic effects of large-scale deforestation by loggers eager for a quick buck in terms of loss of biodiversity. Then followed alarm about climate change due to the carbon dioxide pouring out of fossil-fueled factories, power stations, and automobiles.

We know that trees are the "lungs of the planet" and we need them to live and breathe. Scientists have demonstrated that the world relies on their photosynthesizing power to absorb the so-called greenhouse gases that will otherwise warm the globe's weather systems with potentially disastrous consequences. To help combat climate change, environmentalists are now urging the developed and developing world to commit to help reduce their carbon footprint by initiating programs to plant and protect forests.

City trees

We can all do our part, even if we are far from the great forests that sustain our planet. We can buy lumber from sustainable sources, plant new trees, and appreciate and protect what is already established in urban and rural areas. Trees line our streets, fill our parks and yards, and can even crowd into office vestibules. Even the most modern development plan will include mature trees to offer an oasis of calm and soften the visual impact of glass, steel, and cement. Above all, trees are planted to mark almost every momentous occasion in our lives. In short, trees are as popular as ever.

This book is a celebration of our love of trees. It looks at ways we can each develop a personal link with individual tree specimens that have particular meaning and value.

A New Baby

Surely there can be no greater cause for celebration than the arrival of a new life. Holding a newborn baby in your arms can be one of the most joy-filled and life-affirming experiences in life.

Symbolism

The birth of a baby is a joyous occasion and the planting of a tree symbolizes new life and growth. As the tree matures so will the child. There could be no better lasting record of this new life than establishing another, parallel, living entity. Both grow so fast; take your eyes away for a few weeks, and progress leaps out.

Timing

It is natural to want to plant the tree on the same day as the baptism or naming ceremony, but this may not be practical. Trees fare best when planted in fall or early spring, so it is better to delay celebrating the birth of a winter and summer baby for several months. You could spend the intervening period choosing the most appropriate tree and planning the ceremony itself. Consider planting your tree in a large pot that can be easily brought inside during the winter.

Choice of tree

With so many species, cultivars and varieties available, the choice of tree species is not always easy. It is obviously too early to match a tree to the newborn's character, so it is up to the parents to select whichever seems the most appropriate.

Inspiration

Almost every tree species
has a cultural and spiritual
significance. In Europe, some
cultures link oak trees with
strength and wisdom, while
the mountain ash has links
with Celtic spirituality. People
living in warmer climates
might want to choose a mango
tree, which Hindus believe is
a symbol of attainment and
potential perfection.

Practicalities

When picking a suitable tree,
think about fast-growing
compared with longevity.
Ornamental species, such
as a white-barked birch or
cherry, grow quickly,
matching the new baby, but
a larger, long-lived species,
such as a redwood or hickory,
would still be growing
strongly long after the
child's grandchildren retire.

PLAQUES FOR PLANTING CEREMONIES

It is worth considering incorporating a plaque in your
tree-planting ceremonies, to record the dates, purpose
and tree species for future generations. There are several
options available, but bear in mind that the elements can
be incredibly destructive. Printed descriptions will be
lucky to last more than a couple of winters. Even when
laminated, ink fades while paper yellows. The most
ornate inscriptions carved in hardwood or stone will
usually fill with lichens and frost often shatters ceramic
plaques. The most lasting signage is usually embossed
metal, the letters protruding from the background.
Refresh the sign regularly using wire brushes and a
new coat of paint to keep the message legible.

HOW TO GROW FROM SEEDS

While planting a tree is satisfying in itself, taking it through every stage of its life is even more rewarding. In addition, environmentalists now stress the importance of preserving regional diversity. This means your chosen tree should be of local provenance so that you preserve regional genetic variations and native wildlife, too. And what nicer task than gathering your seeds from nearby woods?

Gathering

- Choose parent trees that are located as close as possible to your eventual planting site.
- Select woodland that is least likely to have been planted by people (avoid commercial woods where all the trees are the same age or planted in straight lines).
- Gather from trees where the same species grow in groups (because the seeds from isolated specimens may be infertile).
- Use buckets or burlap bags for larger seeds, paper envelopes for smaller seeds, and plastic bags for fleshy berries and fruit.
- Gather heavy seeds where they fall (try spreading tarpaulins below to ease the process). The first fruit to drop may be less fertile.
- Use pruning shears to clip off seed bunches.
- Sweep up light or downy seeds from hard surfaces.

Cleaning & storage

- Remove any foliage and husk from the seeds.
- Check carefully for damage.
- Fleshy seeds are intended to pass through the gut of a bird or animal. Emulate this by soaking and mashing, then wash the seeds clean.

- Store cones until they open, then shake them inside a bucket to catch their seeds.
- Most seeds can be safely dried, but heavy seeds, such as acorns, are designed to bury themselves in the leaf mold, so sow them immediately.

GERMINATION

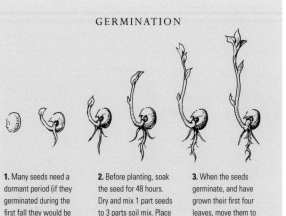

1. Many seeds need a dormant period (if they germinated during the first fall they would be killed by frosts). Store them in a refrigerator for 2–4 months or outdoors.

2. Before planting, soak the seed for 48 hours. Dry and mix 1 part seeds to 3 parts soil mix. Place in a container and spray the soil twice a week to keep it moist.

3. When the seeds germinate, and have grown their first four leaves, move them to a larger pot. Grow them on until they are large enough to transplant.

Seeing a tiny seedling emerge from a dry, wrinkled seed and watching its growth and transformation is a fascinating process.

HOW TO GROW FROM SEEDLINGS

While most tree species can be easily grown from seeds, nature willingly lends a hand. Forest floors are littered with seedlings, all growing in the hope that a storm or lightning strike will create a gap in the canopy that they can exploit. In the absence of natural or man-made intervention, most of these tiny trees are destined to be quickly smothered by lack of light. It is, therefore, usually legitimate to collect these as well as seeds on public land. Always obtain permission from the landowner first if you are on private property.

Why gather seedlings?

- It saves time in terms of storage and germination.
- It speeds up the growing process; even a tiny sapling probably represents a seed that fell from the tree at least a year or two earlier.
- Many seeds have limited fertility—an established sapling should have a far higher success rate.
- Seedlings grow faster than larger trees—in many cases six- month-old "whips" will outstrip much bigger saplings within a few years.
- Bare-rooted seedlings are easier to plant than root-balled trees from nurseries; simply dig into moist ground and heel the sapling in.

Collection

- Gather seedlings after leaf fall (when the sap is down).
- Do not collect when the ground is frozen because this can damage roots.
- Ease the seedling gently from the ground without tearing the bark or roots. Use a fork to loosen the soil if necessary.
- Place the seedlings, roots down, in a large bucket.
- Back at home, label each one immediately and plant in individual pots of moist soil mix or heel into a long trench until late winter.
- Transplant the seedlings to their final location, preferably in autumn or early spring before the sap rises.
- Plant the seedlings densely to promote vigorous upward growth and overcome mortality. This will mimic conditions on the forest floor where generally competition for light and space is strong.
- Protect from pests (*see page 28*)
- Maintain with regular thinning, particularly over the first ten years.

An ash woodland sapling.

PLUM

Prunus spp.

⌒

Man has tapped the rich bounty of many of the dozens of wild plum trees for many thousands of years. Some were chosen for their hard wood and vicious thorns, others for their beautiful spring blossom, but generally it is their fleshy sweet fruit (or drupe) that is the main attraction.

The deciduous *Prunus* family are small to medium trees on average, many of which are defended with sharp thorns, which explains their popularity in hedges.

Blackthorn or sloe is one example. Its Latin name, *Prunus spinosa*, acts as a warning, and the thorns of this fast-growing shrub are so sharp and hard they can puncture a tractor tire. Consequently, it makes an excellent stock barrier. The strong, flexible lumber was once prized for making riding crops and walking sticks, while the astringent hard fruit—too bitter to eat raw—gives a rich almond-like flavor to liqueurs. The damson (*Prunus insititia*) or bullace comes halfway between the thorn and the cultivated plum. It is generally too tart to be eaten raw, but when sweetened with sugar it is perfect for making jams, desserts, or drinks.

Greengages (*Prunus domestica* Reine-Claude group) produce small green or red fruit sweet enough to eat, yet the trees are thorny enough to make a stockproof barrier.

The Myrobalan plum tree (Prunus cerasifera).

EDIBLE & MEDICINAL USE

The cultivated plum (*Prunus domestica*) has by far the fleshiest and sweetest fruit of all. For at least four millennia it has been prized as a delicious fruit, an important source of vitamin C and natural sugars, and, since Roman times, used medicinally for its mild laxative qualities. In its semidried form, it remains a mainstay of Middle Eastern cuisine, while Pruneaux d'Agen are a particular delicacy in southern France. In Central Europe, however, the fruit is most often made into a preserve or distilled as an *eau-de-vie*, known as *slivovitz* in the Czech Republic and *horinka* in Romania.

TREE OF LIFE

People have always had a deeply spiritual relationship with trees. Perhaps this stems from the time when humans first appeared on earth, when our forebears sought sanctuary each night by climbing the branches above the African savanna.

EGYPTIAN MYTHOLOGY

The ancient Egyptian gods Isis and Osiris emerged from Saosis, an acacia tree referred to as the "tree in which life and death are enclosed." Osiris was killed and his coffin was thrown into the Nile, where it became embedded in the roots of a tamarisk tree.

A Tree of Life is often mentioned in Kabbalah and appears throughout Judaic teaching. Jewish yeshivas and synagogues were often called Etz Chaim—Hebrew for "Tree of Life"—and that is also the term for the wooden poles to which the ceremonial Torah is attached. The Book of Genesis also mentions a Tree of Life, while in medieval theology trees repeatedly achieved spiritual significance.

Long before the spread of Christianity, European pagans worshipped trees. The Celts believed that almost all trees contained spirits, but the oak, ash, and thorn were particularly important, followed by fruiting trees such as apples, hazel, rowan, and yew. Indeed, the Christian tradition of planting yew in cemeteries is probably linked to pagan tree worship, because many early churches were built on pagan holy sites. In a similar way, the Vikings worshipped Yggdrasil, "the world tree," which they believed held up the heavens, while apples from a box made of ash fueled the immortality of the gods.

The ancient Celts took the oak's noble presence as a clear sign that it was to be honored.

MESOAMERICAN WORLD TREE

Holy trees also frequently feature in the pre-Columbian cultures of Mesoamerica and are included in Mayan, Aztec, and Izapan carvings at their ceremonial sites. These early cultures believed that world trees, their branches stretching to the four points of the compass, linked their terrestrial realm with the spirit worlds above and below them. The Mayan version was represented by a huge ceiba tree that sometimes depicted the scaly body of an upright caiman. Today, ceiba trees are still revered in many cultures and specimens are often left standing when sections of rainforest are felled.

COMING OF AGE

Most cultures have some type of initiation ceremony or ceremonies to celebrate the change from childhood to adulthood, Christianity's confirmation and Judaism's Bar mitzvah *and* Bat mitzvahs *being examples of such. Within a secular setting, the high school prom, with all its attendant ceremony, can also serve to mark this rite of passage.*

SYMBOLISM

In the past, and in some societies today, the transition to adulthood is associated with legal milestones, when an individual is entitled to vote, marry, or join the military. Yet there is surely a deeper, spiritual aspect to the point when one generation is effectively passing on the baton to the next? The moment can perhaps be better marked by asking the young adult to shoulder responsibility for a young tree, which can then be the focal point for a regular family gathering.

Choice of tree

The species should always be tailored to the individual, but given the impatience of youth, perhaps one which develops quickly is most appropriate.

Birch and ash are fast-growing hardwoods with attractive bark and a pleasing outline. In warm areas, a banyan may be appropriate, because it is fast growing and quick to adapt to new growing conditions.

Inspiration

The fig or banyan tree is
considered sacred in many
eastern religions. It symbolizes
luck, enlightenment, and
interconnectedness. In
Hinduism, it is known as
kalpavriksha, or the wish-
fulfilling divine tree, and the
supreme god Shiva is usually
depicted contemplating in
silence in its shade.

Similarly, the Buddha achieved
enlightenment around
2,400 years ago beneath the
Bodhi tree in Bodh Gaya near
Patna in the Indian state of
Bihar. Although this tree has
long since gone, another was
propagated from a cutting
and a further cutting taken
from that one still lives on.

In Hong Kong, people
consider the Lam Tsuen
Wishing Trees to be very
lucky. At the lunar New Year,
they write their wishes on
pieces of paper and tie them
to oranges before tossing
them into the branches. The
wishes of those that catch on
the foliage and remain there
are meant to come true.

Practicalities

Don't forget a suitable label,
preferably including a name,
a date, and a simple inscription
to mark the occasion (*see page
11*). In many cases, the young
person will be leaving home
to go to college or set up their
own home within a few years,
so a low-maintenance tree
is important. Avoid trees
that need regular pruning
or protection from insects
or nibbling mammals.

A little ceremonial care and
attention during visits home
for college summer breaks
or at regular family reunions,
such as during Thanksgiving,
Christmas, or New Year, can
be a useful focus for bonding
as well as the reflection of the
passing of time.

WILLOW
Populus spp.

The Northern Hemisphere boasts some 400 types of this fast-growing, water-loving tree family. Not surprisingly, the large Salix *family varies widely in appearance. Some, such as the Arctic species, are no more than small shrubs while others grow to over 100 feet (30 m).*

Most species are known as willows, but broader-leaved types are often called sallow, while the whiplike shoots used for weaving are known as osiers. Willows can grow up to 60 feet (18 m) high, but few are forest trees. Most species are cross-fertile and readily hybridize. For example, the weeping willow is a cross between the Peking and white willows. Legend has it that this first arrived in England as the binding around a parcel. The poet Alexander Pope planted the apparently dead string and all British weeping willows are descended from this stock.

For thousands of years, people in China and Europe had chewed the bark of white willow to relieve pain and reduce fever until, in the nineteenth century, its active ingredient, salicylic acid, was isolated and refined to produce aspirin.

Willow bark is very rich in auxins, or plant growth hormones, which explains why willow is so quick to root and layer. Nineteenth-century gardeners learned to water their cuttings with willow bark solutions to promote rooting.

WOOD USES

The timber is relatively spongy and soft, but it has a variety of specialized uses, from basketware to hurdle–making while the soft black charcoal it produces is ideal for drawing. Fishermen once took advantage of its water-resistant qualities to construct their eel traps and lobster pots.

A full-grown white (or Huntingdon) willow (Salix alba).

Willows grow in a range of habitats, but the tree's love of water means it is often found on marshy ground or along rivers where it can stabilize banks and act as a windbreak. It is also increasingly planted in biofiltration beds to purify water courses. Willow trees can grow extremely fast—up to 13 feet (4 m) a year—so despite a high water content, they are increasingly being coppiced as a biofuel.

POPLAR
Populus spp.

*The poplar family has three representatives around the world. The two best-known American examples are the Eastern and Western cottonwoods (*Populus deltoides *and* P. fremontii). One of its European counterparts, its closest relative, is the Lombardy poplar (*P. nigra *'Italica'), which has long been planted along roads to shade work animals. As such, it is an integral part of many of old master paintings by Monet and van Gogh.*

The cottonwoods that snake along the banks of American creeks and levies are so familiar that they need little description. These are one of North America's biggest deciduous hardwoods, with broadly triangular leaves attached to the branches with an off-center stalk that can make them shimmer in the breeze. For all its size, the furrowed gray trunk is weak and often splits, but perhaps the most distinctive feature are the fluffy white seeds that give the tree its name (cotton for clothing comes from the true cotton plant, *Gossypium*, not to be confused with cottonwood trees).

The damp-loving poplars produce poor-quality lumber, yet are widely cultivated commercially because the trees are exceptionally fast-growing, reaching felling age in just 10–30 years. By this stage, they can be a large tree growing up to 130 feet (40 m) tall. The fibrous lumber is cheap and ideal for "one-use" pallets or shipping crates. In Europe, it is used for plywood, matches, and the boxes traditionally used to package soft cheeses, such as Pont l'Évêque and Camembert.

Poplars have an extremely high water content, so prior to felling foresters usually make a deep chainsaw incision in the trunk to drain excess moisture. However, the wood remains full of liquid, which makes it one of the worst timbers to burn (this is due to microscopic pockets of water exploding and spitting on a fire). Even so, it is so fast-growing that it still remains an attractive prospect as a biofuel.

For farmers, however, such considerations are relatively unimportant. To them, the tree is more important as providing quick-growing shelter than for its wood. It is flood- and storm-resistant, and can even right itself after being flattened by hauling on its huge root system.

Lombardy poplars often contribute to a picturesque landscape. Their tall, thin outline creates vertical contrast to horizontal lines.

MONKEY PUZZLE

Araucaria araucana

The common name of this South American evergreen pine comes from a jocular comment. In the mid-nineteenth century, the trees were still novelties in Europe, and as a cultivator showed off his prized specimen, a friend remarked, "It would puzzle a monkey to climb that."

Certainly the tree's form is unusual: a long, typically unbranched trunk, and a tight crown with large, sharp-edge, triangular "needles". Like many conifer trees, the monkey puzzle is extremely hardy and capable of tolerating temperatures as low as -5°F (-20°C).

The monkey puzzle is Chile's national tree. Its natural habitat is the south-central sections of the Chilean and Argentinian Andes, usually above 3,300 feet (1,000 m) where winters are marked by heavy snowfall.

The monkey puzzle's scientific name, *Araucaria araucana*, derives from a local Chilean tribe, the Araucana, who particularly prize the large seeds of the monkey puzzle. Some 200 of these protein-rich, high-calorie seeds develop in each of the female tree's spherical female cones. It has been considered for cultivation, both as a food crop and for its timber, but the tree's commercial potential is hampered by its slow growth: monkey puzzles can take up to a lengthy 40 years to produce their first cones.

FOLIAGE CHARACTERISTICS

Araucaria are tall imposing trees with branches in regular whorls. The thick leaves persist for 10–15 years, and are flat and broad or awl-shaped and curved. Male and female cones are borne on different trees.

The branches have an unusual symmetrical angularity and are completely covered by the stiff, overlapping leaves.

Araucaria is one of the most ancient of tree genera and some specimens of monkey puzzle are believed to be over a thousand years old. Such longevity and the tree's unusual scaly appearance and hardiness made it popular as an ornamental tree with nineteenth-century gardeners and collectors. As a result, it was planted along the west coasts of Europe and North America as well as in New Zealand and southeastern Australia.

HOW TO PROTECT A TREE

Most mature and healthy trees are strong enough to resist attack, which is just as well because spraying or netting off a large tree is rarely desirable or practical. However, young trees are a different matter and are particularly vulnerable to attack from various quarters.

Voles & rabbits

While voles and rabbits can be a problem in very young plantations because they love the tender young shoots, it would be impractical to try to cull the voles. Shooting and trapping rabbits is more realistic, but time-consuming, and while they can be fenced out, this is usually expensive and ineffective. The best solution is generally to protect individual trunks by attaching short plastic guards around the main stem until the trees are too big to be at risk.

Squirrels

These "tree rats" are a major forest pest. Apart from their raids on nuts and fruit, they nibble young bark, killing off new growth, and have a fondness for the "primary" shoot. Once they nip out this tip, the trunk splits and weakens the tree, making it almost worthless for timber. It is impossible to fence out these nimble raiders, and trapping and releasing the animal is illegal in many states, so culling may be the only practical defense.

Deer

Wild deer can also be a serious problem. During spring and summer, they will browse all foliage within reach, but they can be a real menace in late winter when the cold and food shortages make them turn to the high-energy sugary bark. Rutting stags can also damage even substantial trees as they thrash their antlers to mark territories and remove the velvet. Tall trunk guards and high fencing can provide protection, but this is costly and numbers generally need to be controlled. Taste or odor repellents may help. Coating the tree to a height of over 6 feet (2 m) with an egg-and-water mixture or hanging mesh bags containing deodorant soap in the lower branches may help to deter the attentions of deer.

Birds

Many orchards are magnets to birds that find soft fruits irresistible. Dwarf trees can sometimes be defended with netting, but scarecrows, spinning foil disks, and even plastic hawk and owl decoys can deter the worst raiders. At vulnerable times of year, smaller trees can be protected from flying pests and airborne diseases by enclosing them in horticultural fleece.

Wild deer enjoy eating the leafy foliage from small trees.

A NEW HOME

In terms of stressful experiences, experts say moving home is second only to divorce or bereavement. Yet it is also one of life's most significant moments—and never more so than when the new house is someone's first purchase—and a tree, symbolic of putting down roots, is a fine way to mark the event.

PRACTICALITIES

New homes—particularly first ones—are generally temporary. They are also often small, lack yard space, or are in cities, so practical considerations are appropriate. Plant portability is a good idea. For example, a potted shrub can be easily moved from the warmth of an exposed balcony in summer to the protective confines of an apartment in winter. Better still, in due course it can accompany the owner as they move to a bigger urban home—or be transplanted to a country home.

Choice of tree

Lemon and orange trees take well to life in a pot and can be pruned to form interesting shapes. They are also aromatic and produce attractive blossom, not to mention delicious fruit. Alternatively, a bay tree has attractive thick glossy evergreen foliage. In the ancient world, the bay represented success, but today it is more appreciated for its aromatic leaves that perk up Mediterranean,

Middle Eastern, and Indian dishes. The leaves can also be dried to make homemade pot pourri or to imbue clothes in drawers with their delicate scent. In due course, citrus and bay trees alike readily transplant to a relatively frost-free spot, where they will develop into a fairly dense short tree or shrub, providing all the fruit or leaves a chef could desire.

Souvenir

Moving from a much-loved family home can be a truly traumatic event, particularly if it means having to abandon a cherished yard. One way of maintaining a living link with the past is to take a cutting from a favorite tree or shrub (*see page 112*) and transplanting it to the new home. If the symbolic importance of this plant is conveyed to children and grandchildren, cuttings from successive generations of the same plant could be passed on to many descendents. Over generations, one special tree can be cloned and left as a living reminder of a family's growth and movements across countries and even continents.

Inspiration

Johnny "Appleseed" Chapman (*see page 45*) never owned a home, but he entered popular folklore by establishing apple trees across the American Midwest. He collected seeds from the discarded pulp at cider mills and planted seedlings wherever he stopped to preach. He then entrusted the young trees to the care of a local person, funding the process by selling or bartering the stock. This legacy of orchards charted the preacher's wanderings across the Midwest.

HOW TO LAY A HEDGE

Trees have made living barriers since the Iron Age. The oldest hedges were literally whittled from the forest that once stood on either side, but most were deliberately planted across previously open land to demarcate field and estate boundaries during the seventeenth and eighteenth centuries. The popularity of hedges varies throughout the world. While in some countries they are seldom seen, in northern Europe they are used decoratively in backyards as well as being defining features of the landscape.

Most hedges are comprised mainly of thorn trees—left alone, these soon grow tall and block the light getting to the hedge base, creating gaps. A hedge needs to be periodically "laid"—cut back and woven into a living hurdle. This contains stock while providing shelter and food for livestock and wildlife alike.

There are regional variations in hedge style that reflect its purpose. In sheep-farming areas, for example, a hedge is typically low, thick, and thorny. In dairy and beef areas, hedges are thinner and taller, often containing larger trees that can be pollarded to provide fodder and to enable light to reach the understory.

HEDGE LAYING TECHNIQUE

1. Ruthlessly slash back the old hedge, removing all side branches to leave a line of thin, spindly trunks.

2. Cut those closest to the centerline at waist height to provide the "croppers"—the framework around which the living hedge is woven.

3. The remaining trees are the "pleachers." Almost sever their trunks with a diagonal cut to leave a thin hinge of bark and timber just above the soil. Bend them over to point uphill and thread them between the croppers.

4. Drive homemade stakes drawn from the thinnings through the hedge at an angle. These quickly rot away, but not before they have provided vital support to the new growth.

5. Plug gaps with handfuls of thorny thinnings to protect the young shoots that will emerge from the tumbled parent stock next spring.

6. Compress the hedge by forcing it down from the top and then tie everything down by plaiting "heatherings" (long wands of wood or briar) between the stake tops.

Maintain your handiwork by pruning heavily each winter.
With care it will not need laying again for 20–30 years.

ASH

Fraxinus spp.

Members of this large deciduous tree are found in almost every temperate zone around the Northern Hemisphere. There are over 50 species, but the two most familiar and popular are the white ash (Fraxinus americana) of North America and the European ash (F. excelsior).

The common white ash (Fraxinus americana).

The European ash can grow to 65 feet (35 m) or more, which for centuries has made it a valuable landscaping tree. There are several cultivated forms: dwarf, weeping, and with variegated foliage. The southern European flowering ash, *F. ornus*, is more bushy than tall, and it is prized for its scented, creamy flowers in late spring, and leaves that turn a deep purple-red in fall.

It was important to the Vikings who believed the stars hung below the canopy of Yggdrasil, "the world ash," while the ancient Greeks believed meliai were nymphs of the ash, as opposed to the oak's dryads.

The hard pale wood is highly prized. The American species is known familiarly as "tough ash" and its common name comes from the Old English *æsc* meaning "spear". It generally has a very straight grain and turns easily.

Ash is late to come into leaf and sheds its leaves early, prompting the observation in English folklore that the emergence of foliage would foretell the summer weather:

> *Oak before ash,*
> *in for a splash*
> *Ash before oak,*
> *in for a soak*

Detailed analysis of rainfall patterns and observations by amateur naturalists over the past 300 years show there is actually no correlation.

Despite its short growing season, the ash is fast-growing and its winged seeds (or "keys") mean it is often one of the first species to colonize clearings and waste ground. Even when freshly felled, the wood has a low water content (this can be as little as 35 percent in winter). This means it makes one of the best firewoods:

> *Seer* [Seasoned] *or green,*
> *it's fit for a queen!*

MAPLE

Acer spp.

❧

*The world boasts over 150 species of maple, sycamore, or acer, including large specimens such as the Norway maple (*Acer platanoides*)—a common street or park tree—to the spectacularly colorful displays of maple forests in a New England fall. There are also many small, Japanese varieties that make attractive garden features and are popular with bonsai lovers as miniature trees.*

THE COLOR OF MAPLE

Maples are typically medium to large trees, growing up to 150 feet (45 m). The majority of species are deciduous and can be at their most striking in fall, when the leaves turn spectacular shades of yellow, orange, and purple (*see page 108*).

Maples produce winged seeds or "keys", designed to spin like helicopter blades. Strong winds can carry them great distances. Foresters class the family as invasive "pioneers," being among the first to colonize cleared ground.

Although maple wood does tend to be very hard and brittle, the grain can be extremely attractive and the timber resonates very well, making it a natural choice for violins, guitars, and drum casings.

*The sugar maple (*Acer saccharum*), a species native to the forests of northeastern North America.*

For many, the maple is synonymous with Canada. Surprisingly, it has only officially been the country's emblem since 1996, even though it first appeared on the national flag in 1965. Canada produces more than 80 percent of the world's maple syrup, the vast majority coming from Quebec. The syrup comes from half a dozen species of North American maples. The trees prepare for the growing season by producing an energy-rich sap and that of the sugar maple (*Acer saccharum*) is particularly sweet with a sugar content of about 2 percent. Humans harvest this by drilling a hole into the trunk. Each mature tree produces approximately 10 gallons (45 L) of sap every spring. This is then boiled down to make around 1 quart (1 L) of syrup, which is traditionally served on waffles and pancakes.

HOW TO GROW A BONSAI TREE

The Japanese art of growing tiny trees in containers actually began in ancient China. The aim is purely aesthetic, to create a tree in miniature that can be admired in the comfort—and confines—of your own home. This makes it perfectly suitable for modern city life.

Almost any tree or shrub can be cultivated, but most growers favor species with small leaves or needles to create the best visual effect. Maples and conifer species, such as larch, are popular.

To save time, some bonsai starts with a layered cutting (*see page 112*), allowing the grower to encourage rooting on a branch close to side shoots. The cutting starts with a short trunk and branches.

CARING FOR BONSAI

Copper or aluminum wire is wound around branches in order to train them slowly into the desired form. This works best with new growth because the wood is still soft and green. Snipping the trunk, branches, or roots restrains growth. Leaves are selectively removed throughout the year to reveal the tree's form and constant careful pruning is needed throughout the tree's life to manipulate its growth. If properly cared for, bonsai trees can live for many years.

BONSAI PROPAGATION

1. Fill a shallow dish with very light, well-draining, soil—perhaps a mixture of sand and soil mix.

2. Pruning the growing tip of the trunk stunts the growth and makes the tree more compact. Clipping the tips of the branches creates the overall shape. Removing individual leaves helps increase the impression of a tree in miniature.

3. The impression of age can be created by removing bark from a branch to produce a weathered stump.

4. The limited soil dries out quickly, so the tree needs constant watering and light feeding with a fertilizer.

Tools specifically designed for use on bonsai trees play an important role in the maintenance and styling of the trees.

AN ENGAGEMENT

Most early rites of passage are ones over which we have little control—birth and coming of age are, after all, determined nine months before we are born. However, the choice of life partner is a conscious decision that is usually symbolically marked by the exchange of rings and vows. A fitting supplement to these symbols of union would be to plant a tree.

Choice of tree

A pear tree suits the occasion perfectly. Its spring blossom matches the happy mood of the moment, while holding out a promise of things to come. The pear is ripe with the symbolism of fertility and wisdom, while on a practical level it is particularly good for wildlife, attracting a wide range of insects and, in turn, songbirds. It is also quick to produce blossom and pears; even a small tree bears fruit within a year or two.

Alternatively, an ornamental silver birch tree with its pure white bark representing youth and hope might also be a suitable choice. This is a fast growing and relatively hardy tree. The overall effect is incredibly striking with its shimmering foliage in summer, but it is arguably even prettier in winter when it stands out against the muted grays and browns of the surrounding countryside.

Practicalities

While the decision to marry may have been spontaneous, planting a celebratory tree to mark the occasion always requires care and forethought. This is particularly true if this tree is to symbolize enduring love and commitment. So make sure it gets the best start in life. Choose a suitable spot that has a good water supply and adequate drainage. The site also needs to be accessible, not just now, but for regular visits over the coming years. Plant your tree in late fall or in early spring, when the tree is dormant but the ground is frost-free. Protect it from winter gales by giving it a strong stake and guard the trunk from rabbits and deer (*see page 28*). Finally, label your tree with a plaque that will stand the tests of time and weather to be read by your children and grandchildren in years to come (*see page 11*).

INSPIRATION

During the 1560s, the young Mary Queen of Scots would escape her unhappy marriage to Lord Darnley by visiting Melville Castle in Scotland with her Italian secretary, David Rizzio. According to legend, Rizzio marked his love for the queen by planting a Spanish chestnut (*Castanea sativa*) on the banks of the North Esk River. If true, the tree has fared remarkably well and 450 years later is still growing healthily in the castle grounds—a lasting tribute to an ill-fated love.

HOW TO GRAFT A TREE

Many trees that rely on pollination to reproduce do not "breed true." Instead, their seeds contain a jumble of genetic material derived from both the parent tree and the pollinator. This means the seeds germinate to produce a sapling with an unpredictable mix of qualities. This can be a particular problem for fruit and blossom trees. Nursery workers overcome this by grafting.

Grafting entails splicing a twig from a desirable tree onto the roots of another. This means that above the joint the new tree is genetically identical to its parent (the "scion"), while below the ground it mimics the original rootstock. This explains why 'Decio' apple trees, probably one of the oldest varieties in existence, are genetically identical to the seedling believed to have been introduced from Italy by the Roman general Ezio in C.E. 450.

The rootstock likewise brings qualities to the new tree. In particular it determines its size and vigor. Perhaps not surprisingly, limiting growth is now one of the most popular traits required in a world of small yards and high property prices. Thus, for example, regardless of whether a cherry tree is ornamental or fruiting, below ground all dwarf cultivars come from a handful of parent roots.

TREE GRAFTING STEPS

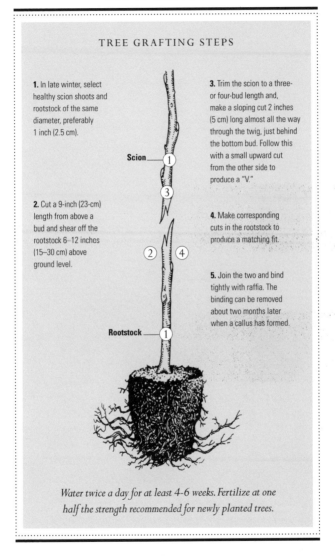

1. In late winter, select healthy scion shoots and rootstock of the same diameter, preferably 1 inch (2.5 cm).

2. Cut a 9-inch (23-cm) length from above a bud and shear off the rootstock 6–12 inches (15–30 cm) above ground level.

3. Trim the scion to a three- or four-bud length and, make a sloping cut 2 inches (5 cm) long almost all the way through the twig, just behind the bottom bud. Follow this with a small upward cut from the other side to produce a "V."

4. Make corresponding cuts in the rootstock to produce a matching fit.

5. Join the two and bind tightly with raffia. The binding can be removed about two months later when a callus has formed.

Scion

Rootstock

Water twice a day for at least 4-6 weeks. Fertilize at one half the strength recommended for newly planted trees.

APPLE

Malus spp.

The apple was first domesticated in Neolithic times and is now one of the world's most widely cultivated deciduous trees. The original wild species, Malus sieversii, *grows in Khazakstan's Tien Shan mountains. Like their familiar cultivated versions (*M. domestica*) these are usually between 15 and 40 feet (5 and 13 m) tall with a spreading crown bearing unusually large fruit for a wild tree.*

*The common crab apple tree (*Malus sylvestris*).*

The seeds from the wild apple do not produce consistent fruit, but the Babylonians learned the technique of grafting some 4,000 years ago. Later, Alexander the Great is credited with introducing dwarf rootstocks to Europe. Grafting allows desirable traits to be sustained and this is how the first cultivated varieties (cultivars) were created.

Since the apple stores well, it was perfect food for early nomads. It may have been planted at stopping points, deliberately and accidentally, long before the first cereals were cultivated. The American pioneer Johnny Appleseed (real name John Chapman, 1774–1845) is famous for helping to tame the West by planting and distributing apple seedlings as he traveled.

The fruit's importance to early agriculture is reflected in many cultures through their myths. One of the twelve labors of Hercules was to pick golden apples from the Tree of Life. In Viking mythology, apples gave immortality to the Norse Gods. Most famously perhaps is the story of man's ejection from the Garden of Eden after Eve succumbed to the temptation of "forbidden fruit."

Today, there are around 7,500 known cultivars worldwide. One of the world's most popular apples is named after an emigrée to Australia, Maria Ann Smith, who found a promising seedling on her Sydney compost heap in the 1870s.

Apples are mainly grown for eating, cooking, and drinking purposes. The soft, aromatic wood of the tree is valued by craftspeople for carving and whittling, while the burning sawdust gives a sweet smoky flavor to food.

BIRCH

Betula spp.

This Northern Hemisphere family of deciduous trees is particularly associated with acidic soils. Birches are one of the principal tree species in the world's largest tract of unbroken forest—the taiga—which encircles the globe across Alaska, Canada, Scandinavia, and Russia.

These are small deciduous trees that grow mainly in cold or temperate Northern Hemisphere regions. They have simple, toothed or pointed leaves, but the principle distinguishing feature is probably the resinous bark, which is often so vividly colored it is referred to in a common name, such as silver birch (*B. pendula*). They have light wispy seeds that are carried by air currents and are quick to colonize any waste ground that is not heavily grazed by deer or livestock.

Most birches are identifiable by their thin, easily peeled, resinous bark, which people have put to many uses since the last Ice Age. Even when the wood is wet, its oils make it highly flammable, and it was a traditional staple in tinder boxes prior to the invention of matches. The fibers could also be shredded and woven into cord or even fabric, while larger sheets of bark made durable writing paper. Native Americans used still larger sections to fashion canoes.

Although the birch is not well known for its edible uses, its sap is widely consumed. Trees across much of northern Europe and Asia are tapped for their sugary juice in early spring. This watery greenish liquid is either consumed fresh or fermented to produce a mildly medicinal light beer.

The bark of the black birch, a species native to North America, is (unlike most birches) rough and dark blackish brown.

TIMBER USE

The timber, though soft, has special uses. It is light colored with an appealing sheen that derives from the natural resins, and its attractive grain makes it valuable as a veneer. Birch has very good resonance, too, which makes it perfect for drums and guitar sound boxes, and some of the world's most expensive speakers.

OLIVE

Olea europaea spp.

This iconic evergreen tree underpins the culture of almost every Mediterranean country, but other olive species are also native to warm temperate and tropical regions of southern Asia and Australasia. It provides oil, fruit, and fine timber, can tolerate drought and is extremely long-lived. It's a tantalizing thought that specimens of olive growing today could have shaded Jesus while he preached or Aristotle as he taught philosophy.

The wild olive tree is short and squat. Its silvery green leaves are oblong in shape, while its flowers are small and white.

TIMBER USE

The olive has dark green, lustrous foliage and rarely grows taller than 50 feet (15 m). Its trunk is usually gnarled and twisted, so although the trunks of ancient specimens can achieve huge diameters, they rarely produce much timber. In spite of this, the hard yellow-green wood has a wonderful grain that is prized by woodturners and cabinetmakers.

It is the fruit of *Olea europaea*, the European olive, that makes the tree so significant to humans. The thin hard flesh is rich in edible oil, one of the principal agricultural products of the Mediterranean region. The olives are green at first and slowly darken to black. Harvesting the green olives begins in late summer with the darkest olives being picked in midwinter. The fresh fruit is bitter and inedible, but a combination of fermentation and pickling for several weeks turns them into the familiar delicacy. The precious oil is extracted by first grinding the fruit to a paste, then squeezing it under high pressure. The highest quality oils are the first to emerge, while those forced out as the pressure increases or by using heat tend to be of lower quality.

The olive tree grows best on alkaline soils, preferably within 35 miles (60 km) of the coast. It depends on hot weather, is very drought-tolerant, and can withstand light frost. It is now cultivated in parts of the world that enjoy a Mediterranean climate, including South Africa, Chile, Australia, and California.

A MARRIAGE

Planting a healthy tree in the ground is perfect for marking the momentous event of getting married. It not only represents hope, growth, and continuity, as the bride and groom embark on their new life together, but also serves as a living reminder of the beauty and strength of the marriage as the years pass.

Practicalities

On the whole, weddings are meticulously planned, which makes it particularly easy to incorporate planting a tree into the celebrations. Clearly it is inappropriate for a white-clad bride or tuxedoed groom to run the risk of getting dirty, but tipping in a ceremonial shovel of soil is still feasible. Better still, with a bit of forethought they could pose for wedding photographs against the backdrop of a flowering cherry planted some months earlier.

Choice of tree

Spring has deep spiritual and cultural links with marriage. This lingers on in today's ritual of throwing confetti, representing flower petals. Perhaps none is more apt than an ornamental cherry, which can display glorious blossom over a prolonged period. An alternative could be a magnolia with its wonderful flowers. These ancient trees have evolved to be pollinated by beetles, so the petals are tough and long lasting. While many of the most striking species come from Asia, others are steeped in the history of the southern states.

Inspiration

Trees growing close together will sometimes naturally conjoin—their branches, trunks, or roots naturally welding together to create a twin-trunked tree with a single canopy. In the past, this was greeted with wonder, particularly when it appeared one tree was putting a branch around another. This was called "a marriage tree," although there are actually two trees. Marriage trees may occur naturally as a result of two branches rubbing against each other, removing the rough outer bark to allow the hormone- and sap-rich inner layers to fuse. However, this union can be encouraged. In a New England tradition, newlyweds plant a tree on either side of the door when building a farmhouse. The trees would be trained together over the lintel to form a "husband and wife tree." It would be easy to do the same today—or train two closely planted cherries to fuse branches.

LOVERS' WALKS

This readiness of trees to bind together also lies behind pleaching, an almost forgotten horticultural art. It was once popular in formal gardens around palaces, where it was used to create private walkways where the nobility could flirt away from prying eyes. The gardeners would plant lines of thin-barked trees such as hornbeam, carefully pruning and interweaving the branches. The bark was then deliberately damaged at the joints and over time would fuse together to make an impenetrable wall of foliage.

HOW A COPPICED
WOODLAND WORKS

Cutting trees to ground level and leaving the stumps to rejuvenate is probably the oldest form of forest management. This drastic technique looks destructive to the uninitiated, but the trees find it enervating—some coppiced stands of small-leaved lime in England's Forest of Dean are believed to be over 7,000 years old. It benefits wildlife too, because it creates a rich mix of trees, shrubs and undergrowth regrowing at varying heights, and the increase in sunlight reaching the woodland floor encourages other plants to flourish.

Some trees coppice better than others. Hazel, oak, ash, chestnut, and beech respond well and produce wood that is useful in small diameters. Traditionally, woods are coppiced in 7- to 15-year cycles. A small woodland area is clear-cut each year, with stumps left protruding from the soil and the roots intact. Once humans have cropped a coppiced site, nature quickly takes over. Seedlings from neighboring mature trees can take root, while the stumps send up suckers. Amid the explosion of new shrub and plant growth in the sun-lit clearing, insect life flourishes, attracting birds, while grazing mammals, such as rabbits and deer, arrive to feast on the tender low foliage if allowed.

Within a few years the stump shoots will have grown to above head height and the canopy has filled in, stifling the understory again.

COPPICING STEPS

1. A section of woodland comprised of young trees, typically 7–15 years old, is selected.

2. The trees are felled leaving a stump protruding a few inches above the soil.

3. Within only a few months shoots sprout from the stump.

4. Within another 7–15 years the trees are the same size as the original and the process restarts.

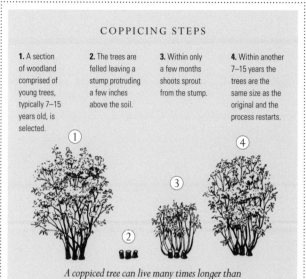

A coppiced tree can live many times longer than if the tree had not been cut down at all.

People, plants, and wildlife then repeat the cycle in the next woodland section.

Historically, the felled trees were processed on-site and nothing was wasted. Smaller hazel withies were woven into baskets and hurdles. Birch and beech twigs might be gathered in bundles with a thicker stave handle to make a broom. Less flexible wood, such as oak, could be split into thin planks and steam bent to produce "trugs" (flat-bottom baskets). Bigger lumber could become fuel, either as logs or stacked upright in cylindrical piles, covered with earth and turf before being fired to make charcoal.

HAZEL
Corylus spp.

The hazel or filbert was one of the first trees to be harnessed by the early hunter-gatherers as they followed the retreating glaciers into Europe 9,000 years ago.

There are over a dozen species of this small (up to 33 feet/10 m) deciduous tree scattered across the temperate Northern Hemisphere. All produce a high-quality protein nut that readily keeps into the depths of winter, but most farmed nuts come from the common hazel (*Corylus avellana*) of Europe or the filbert (*C. colchica*), which originates in the Caucasus. The trees tend to produce a number of trunks from just above ground level. This tendency, coupled with its rapid regenerative powers, make the hazel ideally suited to coppicing (*see page 52*).

Hazel is short-lived—no more than about 70 years— but coppiced trees can live for several hundred years.

The durable timber of the hazel was perfect in the time when flint axes made woodworking difficult and time-consuming. Early settlers found hazels easy to fell to create clearings in the original wild wood that cloaked Europe. The tree's first use was probably as a source of hunting arrows; later its cylindrical thicker boughs made perfect tool handles. Others could be split along their lengths to weave hurdles—or bent over and strung to power the primitive pole lathes on which "bodgers" created crude furniture deep in the woods. The thickest trunks of all were relatively easily cut to length as firewood or chopped to produce the bundle of sticks for the charcoal that fueled the early Industrial Revolution.

The name hazel derives from the Anglo-Saxon *haesel* meaning "cap." This refers to the leaf sheath in which the edible nut develops. This is particularly rich in edible oils. Indeed, in the past Europe's peasantry polished lumber by rubbing a discarded shell vigorously across sanded lumber for a waxy sheen.

The Turkish hazel (Corylus colurna). The male flowers form catkins that grow up to 2 inches (5 cm) long, opening up in February. The tuftlike female flowers grow into hazelnuts.

CHERRY

Prunus spp.

A deciduous native of the Northern Hemisphere, the fleshy sweet fruit of the cherry is frost-sensitive, prone to wildlife raids, has a very short-fruiting season, and does not store well. Despite these factors—or perhaps because of them—it has always been highly prized.

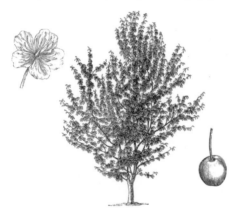

*The wild cherry (*Prunus avium*).*

The trees vary in size from small or medium to large, growing up to 100 feet (30 m) with a symmetrical crown and purplish bark, usually striped with gray/black horizontal batches. They produce white or pink blossoms in winter to spring, and fruit in mid- to late summer.

Cultivated varieties originate from two wild cherries, *Prunus cerasus* and *P. avium* of southeastern Europe. They were first domesticated by the Persians, but it was the Romans who introduced them to Western Europe as their Empire expanded. There are two principal types of edible cherry: the sweet and the sour. The former has a short growing season, keeps badly, and is best eaten fresh. In contrast, sour types (for example, morello cherry) are too tart to eat raw but generally regarded as a far better culinary ingredient.

Although its timber is smaller grade, it has a fine grain and is sought after by woodturners and makers of musical instruments.

Recent research suggests the cherry fruit is a "superfood." A 1-cup (250-ml) serving of juice contains five times more antioxidants than a portion of peas, tomatoes, watermelon, carrots, or banana. These naturally occurring chemicals are proven to help prevent cancer, heart disease, stroke, and aging by reducing harmful free radicals.

FLOWER VIEWING

The trees also produce glorious pink or white blossoms that are revered in Japan's hanami festivals. These start in the subtropical south in late January and end in the mountainous northern in early May. The flowering is so important that television channels broadcast a *sakura zensen* ("cherry-blossom front") that tracks the flowering zone.

VINE

Vitis spp.

At first glance it might seem strange to include the vine as a tree, but this is an important woody plant that can reach the size of a small tree if allowed. The familiar stunted appearance of the plant that people have cultivated for thousands of years is, in fact, due entirely to heavy pruning.

The palmately-lobed leaves of Vitis vinifera *(common grape vine).*

There are around 60 species of vine, but the most famous is probably the wine grape, *Vitis vinifera*, which comes from southern Europe. Its overall shape varies hugely because it is pruned and trained to maximize the light reaching the grapes. Its most distinctive feature, therefore, are its bunches of berries.

The vine, like the olive (*see page* 48), was one of the earliest plants to be cultivated. The sweet fruit of the vine is good to eat fresh and dries readily, but its fermented juice is its most famous and lasting product; winemaking dates back at least 8,000 years. It probably began around the Caspian Sea, where the wine grape is indigenous, but there is evidence from China that it may predate even that ancient beginning. Wine was certainly being produced in Greece by 4500 B.C. and jars of wine were discovered in the tomb of Pharaoh Tutankhamen. Grapes are cultivated on all continents today, both for table and bottle.

Vines are surprisingly hardy, although they only fruit well in areas that enjoy hot summers. They root deeply in search of water. Unpruned, they can grow vigorously, especially when supported, up walls or other trees. This makes them perfect for many smaller gardens where they readily cover trellises to

produce shady corners. In its wild state, the vine would produce an excessive number of buds—between 200 and 300—capable of bearing grapes, which is why they must be pruned to obtain high-quality fruit and enough growth for the next season.

In the nineteenth century, Europe's vineyards were devastated by phylloxera, an insect accidentally introduced from North America. The wine industry was only saved by grafting ancient wine grapes onto phylloxera-resistant roots of an American vine (*V. labrusca*).

FERTILITY

Since the dawn of time, humans have linked trees and fertility. We may no longer worship the life forces that lurk invisibly within every tree, but planting a tree remains a meaningful way of marking the decision to start a family. Planting a tree at the beginning of a pregnancy creates a visible reminder of the baby growing inside the womb. It symbolizes the family's hopes for the invisible new life.

Spirituality

The druids revered the oak and mistletoe as cures for infertility. Later, in pre-Christian times the red-berried evergreen holly and yew symbolized life in the depths of winter—beliefs that persist to this day in Christmas rituals. During the Middle Ages, the Renaissance, and even into the modern age, art and literature are full of allegoric references to forbidden fruits—cherries, figs, and apples—that all represented fertility, sexual innocence, and lust.

Choice of tree

A single fruit tree planted in the center of a lawn may be striking, but harnessing the heat-reflecting and retentive qualities of a wall can make an even more striking way to mark the start of parenthood. Better still, this space-saving form means a small tree can be incorporated into cramped spaces, such as a modern city roof garden. Here, it will produce a curtain of blossom in spring and easily picked fruit in late summer.

INSPIRATION

The mix of beauty and productivity was celebrated for centuries in the formal walled gardens of Europe's palaces and castles. This is perfectly illustrated in the wall-trained fruit tree. Apricots, pears, or cherries were planted next to a south-facing wall, and the trunk and branches were then pruned and trained along a network of wires anchored to the brickwork. This produces a "flat" tree with a pleasant shape—a fan perhaps, a geometric shape, or regular ordered rows of horizontal branches. As well as being attractive, a wall-trained tree takes up minimal space and creates almost no shade. To today's young couples, such techniques are clear demonstrations of the patience, care, and love needed by the perfect parent.

Practicalities

Wall trees use the latent heat trapped in the wall, allowing delicate species to thrive at latitudes where they would otherwise struggle. It is particularly suited to fruit trees, such as apricots, apples, and pears. Almost any size of wall can be harnessed, but it should preferably be south- or west-facing to capture as much sun and warmth as possible. The richer the soil the better, but on roof terraces it is possible to train pot-grown dwarf cultivars in a fan or geometric pattern across even a small wall. Watering and feeding is very important for pot-grown trees as they dry out so much more readily.

HOW TREES ARE FERTILIZED

Keen gardeners are accustomed to helping delicate plants reproduce. Enthusiasts use paintbrushes to pollinate many delicate flowers and to produce hybrids. The sheer size of most trees generally puts these practices beyond direct human intervention, but people have nonetheless been boosting the fertility of orchards and forests for generations.

Pollinating insects are needed for fruit on most flowering trees.

Many trees, such as apples, pears, and cherries, are not self-fertile, which means that they require cross-fertilization from another tree of the same species. Nursery workers overcome this by planting groups of trees that will blossom at the same time.

Insects are vital to fertility. While many trees reproduce asexually, most fruit, nut, and drupe production relies on insect pollination. Wild flies and bees, hoverflies, moths, and butterflies all play a part. Domesticated honey bees are usually far more important due to the sheer numbers involved. While bumblebee colonies may number just 20 or 30 individuals at the end of summer, a typical hive has 20,000–50,000 workers and, better yet, it is portable.

Beekeepers are critical to modern orchards and forestry, moving their hives around the countryside to coincide with blossoming of major crops. Hives may be installed in apple orchards in spring, then be moved to fruit farms before transferring to heather hillsides later in the year.

Many of the world's 850 fig species can only be pollinated by one insect species. Each "fruit" has an entrance hole shaped to admit just one wasp species. When European figs were first introduced to North America, the trees failed to reproduce viable seeds until their specific pollinating wasp was introduced.

WEATHER-DRIVEN POLLINATION

Some trees eschew insect help, relying instead on the elements. This is particularly true of species that grow in cold climates where insects are much less prevalent in the flowering season. Hazels, willow, and birch, for example, produce their familiar catkins or "lambs tails" in late winter and rely on the wind for pollination.

FIG

Ficus spp.

❧

There are some 850 species of the Ficus *family. Many are parasitical and classed as "stranglers", relying for support on another tree, which is then slowly smothered, while others are little more than spindly shrubs. Despite this, figs are critical to the cultures of ancient Egypt, Greece, and Rome and remain central to many eastern religions.*

The fig is the first plant specifically mentioned in the Bible, it is listed as an approved food in the Torah, and there is a chapter named after it in the Qu'ran. Buddha is said to have found enlightenment while meditating under a sacred fig, *Ficus religiosa,* and the species is the "world tree" of Hinduism.

During the Punic Wars, Cato the Elder used a basket of ripe Carthaginian figs to demonstrate to the Senate the proximity of the rival empire to Rome as he argued in favor of war in 149 B.C.

Humans find most varieties of fig inedible, but many wild species are vital to the rainforest food chain. A notable exception is the common fig, *F. carica,* believed to be indigenous to western Asia and cultivated by humans throughout the Mediterranean for thousands of years. Commercial fig orchards have been established in other subtropical regions, including California. Fig trees are also a feature of larger yards (mature specimens can grow up to 50 feet / 15 m), prized for

The common fig tree's foliage and fruit.

their glossy deciduous foliage and muscular branches as well as succulent fruit. In fact, that "fruit" is actually a flower that both blooms and seeds inside a fleshy coating. It is very nutritious, and although rich in natural sugars, it is one of the highest plant sources of calcium, fiber, and anti-oxidants. It dries well, which made it a perfect food for early nomadic farmers long before grains were domesticated.

CULTURAL SIGNIFICANCE

The fig has long been associated with fertility. It is thus ironic that its leaves have been used prudishly to cover the genitalia of classical statues—usually long after the carving was made. This may be because Adam and Eve covered their nakedness with fig leaves after eating the forbidden fruit in the Book of Genesis.

COCONUT PALM

Cocos nucifera

The oversize seeds of this large swaying palm, found growing on tropical sandy shores, are particularly buoyant and salt-resistant. This means the tree can harness the ocean currents to distribute its seeds, thereby colonizing virtually every coast throughout the tropics—much to the advantage of the people living there.

The coconut palm (Cocos nucifera)*.*

Cocos nucifera is a tall, thin-trunked tree that grows up to 100 feet (30 m) high and is topped with a fringe of spiky palms. The nuts nestle at the bottom of these, with each tree producing up to 75 coconuts per year.

Almost every part of the tree has a use. The coconut (not a true nut, but a drupe or pit surrounded by tissue) contains a pithy white edible flesh. This is high in saturated fat (at 90 percent, it exceeds animal fats such as butter) and trace elements such as iron, zinc, and phosphorus. When grated and mixed with hot water, it produces a "coconut milk" that forms an essential ingredient in Asian cuisines.

The shell is the hardest part of the tree and is often used to make bowls. A fine pore structure lets it produce a high-grade activated charcoal, which makes it particularly

effective in absorbing gases and impurities, and indeed gas masks have been made out of coconut shells.

The stringy outer husk, or "coir," is also valuable. It can be shredded to produce a coarse fiber that can be woven into rope, cloth, or doormats, or compressed to make fuel briquettes or composted to create a growing medium.

Palm fronds are useful to local communities. When placed over a wooden frame, they give basic protection from the elements, or individual leaves can be woven to make baskets and matting. The rib of the leaf can be peeled and separated to produce durable, thin skewers that can be turned into fishing hooks or arrows.

Palmwood from the trunk can be used for furniture making instead of threatened tropical hardwoods.

ANCIENT FARMING

Unlike modern agriculture, which favors large single-crop fields of crops or grass, our ancestors saw trees as an integral part of food production.

Cockspur-thorned hawthorn (Crataegus crus-galli).

Hedges have been used to enclose livestock since Bronze Age farmers first cleared woodland to create fields (*see page 52*). It is possible to date a hedge by counting the number of tree species it contains: for each species the hedge is roughly a century old. Early farmers used any seedlings that were on hand (boosted by later "colonizers"), so a hedge containing over ten species is probably a thousand years old, whereas a 300-year-old "enclosure hedge" was planted methodically with nursery stock so it typically contains just three or four.

Until the Middle Ages, peasants were allowed "pannage" in the royal hunting forests of Britain and Europe. Every fall swineherds were allowed to turn out their pigs into the forest to feed on acorns and beechmast, risking the unwanted attention of wild boar and wolves.

Seminomadic tribes have cultivated forests using "slash and burn" farming for millennia. Trees are felled and the brush burned to create a nutrient-rich clearing, which is cultivated until the soil is depleted. The humans then move on to allow natural regeneration to return the site to forest. On a small scale this practice is perfectly sustainable—

unlike modern clear-cutting of huge areas to create grazing or arable fields.

Until recently, farmers pollarded trees by "topping" the trunk above head height. This is like coppicing (*see page 52*) but enabled new shoots to spring from the stump, out of reach of livestock. In due course, these shoots were harvested for tool handles and firewood, while the foliage would fatten grazing animals before the winter cull.

Bees have been domesticated in Europe and North America for centuries, but wild honey is collected in Africa, Asia, and South America. Hunters clamber high up into the forest canopy using ladders and ropes to subdue a bee colony with smouldering tinder before plundering its nest of its sweet cargo.

HEALTH

Experiencing a health scare always makes us reevaluate our priorities. A brush with cancer or heart disease reminds us only too forcefully of the tenuousness of human existence.

Symbolism

Once the scare is over, there is little so life-affirming as to establish and nurture a new life. It can be powerfully healing to watch a slender sapling slowly thicken and put on leaves as if mirroring our own slow recovery. There is also a curiously primeval aspect to the act, something that resonates with the ancestor who wondered at apparently dead twigs springing back into life each spring or the druid who worshipped in a sacred grove.

Inspiration

Western medicine usually traces its birth to Hippocrates of Kos, who is frequently described as the father of medicine. He was the first physician to separate medicine from religion. Instead of blaming ill-health on the gods' displeasure, he argued that disease stemmed from diet and lifestyle.

Hippocrates taught under a plane tree on the Greek island in the fifth and fourth centuries B.C. Paul of Trasus was also said to have preached under the same tree. A huge 500-year-old plane still grows on the site, which local legend claims is a direct descendant.

The Kos islanders are staunchly Greek Orthodox in faith, but to this day they hold an annual ritual that reeks of a pagan past. In late summer, local women make wreaths from the leaves of the plane tree. Then the previous year's wreath is thrown in the sea and the people "baptize" the new wreath in its waters before clasping Hippocrates' tree for strength and long life.

Modern resonance

The symbolism has echoes further afield, stretching even into establishments of medical science. Seeds and cuttings from Hippocrates' tree have been sent all over the globe. One was planted in the grounds of the United States National Library of Medicine in Bethesda, Maryland, while others have found their way to the grounds of medical schools at universities around the world: Yale, Michigan, Alabama, Glasgow, Sydney, and Victoria.

Choice of tree

A plane is ideally suited as a planting project for someone slowly returning to full health. And if there is any hint of superstition and humoring the gods in planting a plane, at least the invalid is in excellent medical company.

The obvious alternatives would be trees with medical uses. Willows are vigorous with a bark that was the original source of aspirin, while many species of eucalyptus are similarly fast-growing and provide essential oils. Finally, for the very patient and forward-thinking, to this day yews remain the primary source of taxanes, which are valuable anticancer drugs.

HOW TO KEEP
YOUR TREES HEALTHY

All too often trees are left to their own devices after planting. Many survive and thrive, but, like all living organisms, most benefit from continual care and attention.

In many ways, a sapling is like a child, ––it needs protection from the elements and unwanted attention. Like any fast-growing thing, a sapling needs plenty of food and water to stay healthy.

Individual trees can also stifle their own growth. In-growing branches and shoots block out light from the center of the canopy, and crossing branches rub against each other. Prune these branches judiciously to encourage growth outward and to maintain a good shape.

It is easy to underestimate how much water a new tree needs. Water the planting hole well, then soak again once the tree is in its hole. If the water does not drain away easily, choose a tree that can cope with waterlogged soils.

Cut dead, diseased, or weak branches out neatly and treat the wound against infection. While healthy trees can often fight off attack, be vigilant for serious pests and diseases and treat accordingly. Fruit needs close attention if the crop is to be worthwhile; look out for birds and other animals that may raid the harvest before you. Deer and small mammals can nibble young shoots and bark, and kill a tree that is not protected (*see page 28*).

STAKING & MULCHING

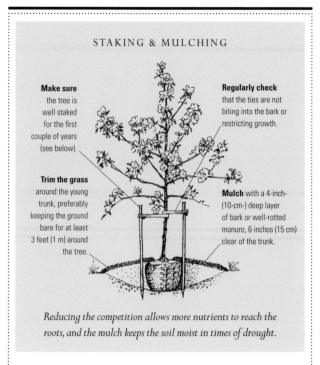

Make sure the tree is well staked for the first couple of years (see below).

Regularly check that the ties are not biting into the bark or restricting growth.

Trim the grass around the young trunk, preferably keeping the ground bare for at least 3 feet (1 m) around the tree.

Mulch with a 4-inch- (10-cm-) deep layer of bark or well-rotted manure, 6 inches (15 cm) clear of the trunk.

Reducing the competition allows more nutrients to reach the roots, and the mulch keeps the soil moist in times of drought.

PLANTING & AFTERCARE

It is a common mistake to plant to deeply, which can lead to rotting of the trunk and tree failure. Plant so that the topmost roots are just under the soil. Keep new trees well watered during their first two years. Trees in pots will benefit from an annual feed, regular watering year-round, and fresh soil every two years.

EUCALYPTUS

Eucalyptus spp.

There are over 700 eucalypti, all but nine of which are native to Australia where they form the backbone of the nontropical woodland. They are commonly known as gum trees, in reference to the oily sap produced by many species. On hot days, the volatile sap vaporizes to imbue the landscape with a characteristic blue haze.

There are three main types of gum. Forest trees have a tall single trunk with a relatively high, small crown. At over 325 feet (100 m) *Eucalyptus regnans*, or Australian mountain ash, is the tallest of all flowering plants, topped only by the sequoias (*see page 104*) of North America's Pacific coast. Woodland trees form a large canopy and branch lower down. Mallees are multistemmed short trees or shrubs and dominate the arid landscapes of the Australian Bush. Many species are now cultivated all over the world for the ornamental properties and valuable timber, notably throughout the Tropics.

Most eucalypti are evergreen, although many shed their leaves, particularly during the dry season to conserve water. Although the trees are native to the Southern Hemisphere, their speed of growth and drought-tolerance has led to their being extensively planted across many parts of Africa and Asia. In arid areas, they provide welcome shade and can help prevent salination.

Eucalyptus flowers provide copious amounts of nectar for insects, birds, bats, and possums, which act as pollinators. The aromatic oils are easily refined from the foliage and widely used as a decongestant, a natural insecticide, and a cleaning agent. Most herbivores cannot tolerate the oil compounds, but koalas and possums are able to feed on the leaves. However, the oils are slow to break down in the thick litter of leaf and bark that builds up in eucalypti forests. This litter easily ignites and devastatingly hot bush fires can rapidly spread through the oil-rich air. The trees themselves are adapted to survive by regenerating from roots and fire-resistant seeds, but humans and wildlife can suffer badly.

Eucalyptus robusta, *commonly known as swamp mahogany, is a tree native to eastern Australia.*

WOLLEMI PINE

Wollemia nobili

Until recently the last known members of the primitive Wollemia genus were two million year-old fossils (the oldest versions date back 200 million years). This changed abruptly in 1994 when a ranger, David Noble, stumbled across 100 mature living specimens in a rainforest gorge in the Wollemi National Park in the Blue Mountains near Lithgow, 150 miles (240 km) from Sydney, Australia.

What greeted him was a medium tree that had survived 17 ice ages, and its discovery can be described as the botanical equivalent of the coelacanth. It is the only living member in its genus. Although it is often called a pine, the tree's foliage actually looks much more like a fern and it has an unusually knobbly bark.

Since the discovery, the precise site has been kept a closely guarded secret. This is critical because there are fewer than 100 specimens in the wild, growing in three small pockets in isolated gorges. DNA analysis suggests that these stem genetically from just one or two individuals, which makes them particularly vulnerable to extinction.

Fortunately, unlike most conifers, the trees have a remarkable ability to self-coppice by spontaneously sprouting multiple trunks from their base. As a result, conservationists are now cultivating thousands of saplings around the world to protect the plants from accidental extinction. These saplings are now being sold to raise funds and to reduce the novelty value of the wild trees to plant poachers.

SIZE & GROWTH HABIT

The Wollemi pine can grow to 130 feet (40 m), with a trunk diameter of almost 3 feet (1 m). Despite coming from a subtropical climate, it tolerates temperatures ranging from 23°F to 113°F (-5°C to 45°C), but grows quickly—almost 2 feet (60 cm) in a year— on slightly acidic soil with plenty of light.

Wollemi pine is a "living fossil" whose evolutionary line was thought to be long extinct. The oldest Wollemia fossil has been dated to 200 million years ago.

HOW THE AGE OF A TREE IS CALCULATED

Trees change shape and appearance as they age. People have long known that a tree's age can be determined by counting the distinct growth rings across the trunk. Each ring represents a year's growth. The pattern of radiating bands is most pronounced in trees living in temperate zones where the weather has more distinct seasons, whereas in tropical rainforests there tends to be little change throughout the year.

Early in the twentieth century an American astronomer, A. E. Douglass (1867–1962), invented the science of dendrochronology when he correctly predicted historic climate patterns (and solar activity) would be reflected in tree rings. He demonstrated how a damp, warm year will produce a wide ring, while a drought results in a very narrow band. Occasionally, a particularly bad summer means the growth ring is absent. In other words, the ring pattern is effectively a bar code and can be "read" against a scientific database of tree cross sections. Scientists can tell how old a tree was when it was felled, and can even determine exactly when it was growing at any point over the past 26,000 years.

Growth rings are most easily viewed by taking a horizontal cross section through the trunk. This is possible with a fallen tree but not a method to contemplate with a prized veteran. One method is to bore a small core sample through the trunk, but this still involves damage to the tree and will not work with hollow specimens.

The definitive answer is to carbon date a small sample of timber. The reliability of this technique was first proved by testing wood from an ancient Egyptian barge whose precise age was already known from hieroglyphs. When any plant turns water and gas into sugar, a small proportion of the carbon dioxide will be the mildly radioactive carbon-14. This slowly decays as soon as it becomes plant tissue, so by measuring the wood's radioactivity, scientists can tell when the tree grew.

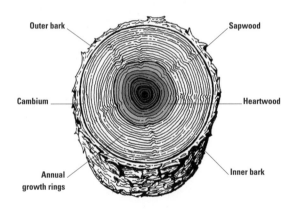

These bands are the result of each year's spurt of new growth. The inner, lighter ring is formed in spring when growth is comparatively rapid. The outer part, or "summer wood," is denser and darker because it is produced more slowly.

New Beginnings

*Most of us experience dramatic upheavals in our lives—
momentous points where we suddenly embark on a
completely new path. This is often unexpected and painful—
for example a divorce or layoff—with all its attendant
heartache and uprooting of possessions and routines.*

Alternatively, a new start may stem from an entirely positive choice. Many people make dramatic career changes by retraining, becoming self-employed, or moving many miles to take on a new challenge.

Such moments do create a natural opportunity to pause and think about both the past and the future. This is the time to make fresh resolutions and to take new vows. The best of intentions can easily slip, and planting a tree can establish a living reminder to keep to the straight and narrow. As time dims the memory of the traumatic or challenging events that lie behind its planting, the steady growth and constant presence of the tree will serve as a constant *aide-memoire*.

Inspiration

The Anishinaabeg peoples from the Great Lakes revere the eastern white cedar. Its wood was whittled and bent to make the frames of their birch bark canoes, and its twigs were scattered on the fire to produce a fragrant smoke. This had a symbolic purifying role—a form of spiritual deep-cleanser.

Choice of tree

What better way to turn over a new leaf than to mark a change with a white cedar? Better still, it is also well-suited to modern backyards. It is comparatively fast-growing, yet small (normally growing to no more than 60 feet / 18 m). Despite this, at 1,350 years, cedars that grow in Southern Ontario are the oldest trees in Northeast America. In other words, it should long outlast even the most momentous change of direction yet remain a thing of permanent beauty.

An alternative could be to set a visionary goal. This is no time for the impatience of youth, but instead a time to show a real long-term commitment to the future by planting a long-lived, slow-growing tree, such as a sequoia, oak, or olive.

Neither you nor your heirs might be there to see it reach full maturity, but it is a concrete demonstration of faith in the new turn that life has taken.

Practicalities

Location is particularly important for such a private gesture. The tree should be planted in a secluded spot where you can retire to meditate quietly, away from intrusion. Also, unlike many ceremonial trees, this is a deeply personal living monument. It is a reminder to the individual, not to the world, thus no public explanation in the form of a plaque is needed.

In some cases, however, it is appropriate to place a small label marked with the date and initials—a cryptic marker with which to intrigue a passerby in years to come.

HOW TO ENCOURAGE WILDLIFE

*Trees are beautiful in their own right, but their appeal is
enriched by the wildlife they attract. The creatures that
live and feed in and around woodland have been described
as forest makeup or jewelry. There are some simple ways of
attracting a diverse wildlife.*

Add variation

Avoid planting single species
in regimented blocks. Instead
establish a mixture of trees,
scattering blocks of the same
species to mimic the way
saplings naturally group
around the parent tree.

Try to plant indigenous
varieties because these
are best for native wildlife.
Ideally, mix fast-growing
colonizers (such as birch,
maple, and ash) with fruit
(rowan and wild cherry)
and slow-maturing
dominant hardwood
species (oak and beech).

Shelter & food sources

Broad-leaved deciduous trees
generally provide better
habitats, but evergreen
conifers (particularly native
species) provide valuable
shelter in winter and their
cones are an important food
for birds and mammals.

Shelter is important, too.
Veteran trees provide natural
cavities, but these will be
lacking in young woodland.
To add to the wildlife appeal
of a young wood, provide a
variety of sizes and designs of
bird and bat boxes and hang
them at a range of heights

A barn owl tree box.

on larger trees. Fill smaller weatherproof containers with corrugated cardboard to make ideal hibernating quarters for insects. Place wooden boxes on the ground and cover with branches and leaves to attract natural pest controllers.

Mature woodland usually offers plenty of wild food, so while saplings are becoming established provide feeding stations, set at various heights. Variety is key if you are to attract different species. Successful stations will inevitably catch the attention

of predators, so site them close to cover. Opportunists, such as squirrels and crows, can monopolize the food sources, so control these or use mesh to exclude these bullies.

Woods require careful management, but when thinning and pruning, avoid undue tidiness. Leaving piles of branches to rot creates food for invertebrates, such as beetles, which in turn provide food for birds. The tangle of branches will also provide shelter for reptiles and mammals.

LARCH
Larix spp.

There are about a dozen members of this hardy coniferous genus distributed across the colder regions of the Northern Hemisphere. The tree grows at mid- to high altitude in the mountains of Europe and Central Asia and is one of the main species found in the vast taiga forest that clad the boreal lowlands below the Arctic Circle.

FOLIAGE LOSS

The most striking feature of the larch is that it is a deciduous conifer, shedding its needles each fall to conserve moisture. Its bark has a rusty tinge and the cones are relatively small, clinging to the branches long after the clusters of needles have dropped.

Many creatures depend on the larch. In the cold climes where it thrives, the tree is the sole food of several species of moth, while in winter squirrels and birds, such as the nutcracker, rely on its cones for food. Birds of prey, such as the northern goshawk, favor the tree as a nest site, benefiting from the ease of access through the bare branches in late winter, but later valuing the foliage for privacy, and using its small twigs and resinous needles as a natural pest-repellent lining for their nests.

The larch is one of the principal species for bonsai (*see page 38*) because its delicate needles and knobbly bark naturally mimic large ancient trees. The fresh timber is a distinctive orange due to the resinous sap that acts as a natural preservative. Its excellent rot- and waterproof qualities mean that larch timber is extensively used for yacht building, and farmers use it for fencing in damp areas. Its straight, knot-free grain and attractive appearance make large trees (some grow to 164 feet/ 50 m) a valuable timber crop. Larch is grown across North America and Europe, where it is an important timber for building construction and paneling, particularly in central Europe.

The European larch (Larix decidua) is a species of larch native to the mountainous regions of central Europe. It is very cold tolerant, able to withstand temperatures as low as -50°F (-45°C).

RUBBER TREE

Hevea brasiliensis

In 1876, an Englishman, Henry Wickham, penetrated the heart of the Amazon rainforest to steal its most jealously guarded secret. His prize was a tree that can grow to 140 feet (42 m) in the wild with glossy green leaves, a relatively smooth brown bark, and a sticky white sap—latex. Brazil had the monopoly on the production of this natural rubber, which had been harvested for at least 3,000 years by the people of Mesoamerica and which was becoming increasingly important as the industrialized world.

Most of the seeds smuggled out by Wickham perished, but some germinated and were sent to Sri Lanka and Malaysia. Commercial plantations in Southeast Asia slowly came to dominate the rubber trade over the next 60 years, until neoprene, a synthetic rubber, was developed in the 1930s.

Natia, the finest wild Brazilian rubber, is still harvested from widely spaced wild trees by licensed tappers and is one of the least destructive ways of exploiting the rainforest. Trees grow quickly and are first tapped at around six years and continue to be productive until they are 25 years old.

Tapping involves using a sharp knife to remove a thin layer of bark from which the sap oozes out. It is thought that the latex is the tree's natural defense against predation by insects.

Until recently, the tree's timber was largely ignored, but rubber wood has begun to be used for furniture and toys. It has a dense grain, an attractive color, and minimal shrinkage. It is generally regarded as environmentally friendly because it is almost always harvested from commercial plantations when the trees have reached the end of their latex-producing life, rather than virgin rainforest.

Sap being collected from a tapped rubber tree plantation. Progressively higher cuts are made, allowing the trees to be tapped for several years.

HOW TO COMBAT
CLIMATE CHANGE

Most scientists now agree our burning of fossil fuels coupled with large-scale forest destruction are contributing to significant climate change. As carbon dioxide levels rise, so do average temperatures around the globe. Some predictions suggest the increase could be as much as 5°F (3°C) by the end of the century.

This has led environmentalists to urge consumers to redress their fossil fuel use by planting trees. Indeed, many industries that are perceived to be polluting (such as airlines) offer customers the chance to participate in carbon offsetting programs. Unfortunately, some of these have been unmasked as scams. In some cases, trees were not planted or consumers were simply paying for existing projects.

Conscientious consumers can still use trees to repair some of the damage. Buying patches of remaining rainforest helps to protect it for future generations, while contributing to aid projects that supply seedlings to the developing world can help prevent desertification as well as generating valuable sources of food, fuel, and shade.

Closer to home, planting your own trees ensures genuinely new areas of woodland are created. If space is sparse, establishing hedges instead of fences creates a living barrier that is a valuable wildlife resource.

Hedges provide important shelter and protection for wildlife. They are a better choice of boundary than fences or walls, especially if native trees and shrubs are used.

However, planting can only ever be a small part of the equation, because when trees die or rot they release the carbon that they locked away when living. At the very least, this latent energy should be captured in the form of heat on a wood-burning stove or boiler or composted to make peat-free growing mediums.

The best solution of all may be to remove the wood as lumber and build with it, in order to lock away the greenhouse gases for centuries rather than for decades. In fact, were this thinking to be applied on a wide scale, it would effectively convert our towns and cities into "frozen" forests.

PROSPERITY

There are times in many people's lives when it is reasonable to feel self-satisfaction. After the children have left home and school, the mortgage has been paid off, and the business is going well, then it is a good point to sit back and reflect.

An arboretum—a collection of trees—is a fitting way to mark a successful career. It is a living embodiment of the vision of its creator that reflects his or her imagination, and also leaves an enduring mark on the landscape to be admired by future generations.

Inspiration

The great industrialists of the nineteenth century often chose to plant exotic and beautiful trees from around the world. These were carefully established to mix colors, sizes, and shapes, often landscaped around water features. The idea, of course, was to create a beautiful place in which to stroll and impress friends and neighbors.

The idea appealed to the great entrepreneurial drive of the age. It demonstrated a mastery of the natural world—trees gathered on the other side of the world brought back and tamed in great parks or estates. These arboreta were also frequently the result of grand experiments—to investigate whether there was commercial potential in non-native species.

Innovators

Sometimes great discoveries
stemmed from these
pioneering collections.
Redwoods from North
America's Pacific coast, for
example, thrive in the mild
climate of Britain's west coast.
In Scotland there are four
Douglas firs topping 200 feet
(60 m), all planted on estates
by men whose fortunes were
built on American trade.
Charles Sargent (1841–
1927) was the son of a
wealthy Boston banker
who converted the family's
estate into a 130-acre
arboretum. The results
so impressed the nearby
Harvard academics that
in 1872 they invited him
to become director of
the University's Arnold
Arboretum. He came of age
as a dendrologist, and for the
next 55 years, extensively
researched North America's

trees and fought tirelessly
to preserve her forests,
particularly in the Catskills
and Adirondacks. A white
spruce is planted in the
grounds of the Massachusetts
State House in his memory.

Choice of tree

It is a lesson we could learn
from today. What better
way to celebrate wealth
and happiness than with a
stand of mighty Pacific Coast
conifers? For those with a
grander vision, what about
a nineteenth-century-inspired
collection of exotic species?

If taking this path, make
sure to select a broad range
of heights, forms, and colors.
Consider not merely the
foliage, but the bark and the
tree's shape in winter—and
preferably plant carefully so
trees complement each
other across the seasons.

HOW TO USE TIMBER
RESPONSIBLY

Humans have relied on wood as a raw material since the dawn of time. Since the nineteenth century, its use has declined in favor of steel, concrete, plastics and glass, largely because architects saw these as stronger and more uniform than lumber. Its fall from fashion was compounded by concerns about irresponsible logging in the world's dwindling rainforests. More recently, technical improvements and concerns about global warming have begun to turn the clock back.

Provided forests are replanted after felling, timber is the ultimate sustainable building material. It is less energy-consuming than concrete and steel, and it locks away carbon dioxide as it grows. Wood also looks more "natural," fitting in with modern thinking that stresses environmental care.

There remain good reasons to be wary of tropical hardwood. Much of this comes from illegal or nonsustainable logging. The international Forest Stewardship Council has a certification plan to guarantee the provenance of legitimate wood—look for their "tree check" logo.

Source lumber as locally as possible to reduce transport emissions, generate income in nearby woodlands, and help to pay for their upkeep and health. Most developed nations also insist on sustainable management.

Modern lamination techniques form huge beams from smaller cuts of lumber. This advance is important because the demand for large lumber has outstripped supply. By gluing smaller pieces of lumber with modern adhesives, it is possible to make beams that are stronger than a solid wood equivalent.

Similarly, new technologies such as acetylation (which reduces lumber's capacity to absorb and release water) can create materials that are as stable, predictable, and durable as steel or concrete. It is worth exploring all options before selecting scarce hardwood.

Look for new wood products rather than solid lumber. Softwoods can be processed to create new materials such as medium-density fiberboard (MDF), a mix of wood fibers, wax, and resin, which is pressed into panels.

Adding a lumber structure to your yard is guaranteed to create impact, and is beneficial for the environment, too.

EBONY

Diospyros spp.

Ebony is the general name given to about 450 tropical deciduous and evergreen trees that produce a dense black heartwood and a fleshy, somewhat tart fruit, the persimmon.

The best timber, called Ceylon ebony, comes from *Diospyros ebenum*, an evergreen that grows to 70 feet (21 m) tall. It is native to Sri Lanka and India, but there are also important species in Africa, Australia, South Asia, Hawaii, and the Americas.

All ebonies grow extremely slowly; the heartwood can take over a century to develop. However, once mature, it is one of the densest of all timbers (it sinks in water) and consequently very strong. Characteristically, it is jet black, although some species are streaked with yellow, and it is commonly known as the wood used to make chess pieces, piano keys, and violin fingerboards.

The ancient Greeks knew the persimmon as the date-plum or "fruit of the gods" (in fact, the scientific name for the genus, Diospyros, means literally "god's wheat"). It was probably the lotus fruit mentioned in Homer's Odyssey that was so delicious that those who ate it forgot about returning home. It is still particularly highly prized in Japan, China, and Korea, where it is often dried and eaten as a delicacy.

PERSIMMON FRUIT

The Japanese species (*D. kaki*) is the most widely cultivated. Although native to China, it was introduced to Europe and California in the nineteenth century. It is extensively grown in Israel and often marketed as Sharon fruit. The fruit's color varies by cultivar from light yellow-orange to dark orange-red. It is rich in tannins, making it astringent when unripe, but it ripens to a sweet pulpy flesh. The American persimmon (*D. virginiana*), or "simmons," contains more vitamin C and calcium than the Japanese species.

*The North American persimmon tree (*Diospyros virginiana*) is an elegant tree with rugged bark. The fruit is very bitter before it is fully ripe.*

WALNUT

Juglans spp.

Walnuts have a long association with man and almost every part of this deciduous tree is prized. The edible nut is actually the kernel that grows inside a dense green fleshy coating. Botanically, it is a drupe rather than a nut (other drupes include cherries, mangoes, and coconuts).

The deciduous *Juglans* genus contains about 20 species that are scattered across the Northern Hemisphere and into South America. The tree is valued both as an ornamental and for its commercial qualities. The two most important species are *J. regia* (Persian or English walnut) and *J. nigra* (black walnut). They are deciduous hardwood trees, related to the ash, with palm-like gray-green leaves that give them a curiously airy appearance, particularly when growing alone.

The tree is famous for its fruit. Walnuts are rich in a fine edible oil that has long been prized in Middle Eastern, French, and Italian cookery. Both the nut and the oil work particularly well in salads and as an accompaniment to cheese.

The wood is dark and hard and its grain polishes to a wonderful sheen. The black walnut tree is very highly valued for its veneer and lumber, and is in fact the most commercially important lumber in many parts of the United States.

*The common or Royal walnut (*Juglans regia*).*

The walnut tree produces a natural herbicide, juglone, which can stunt or even kill plants in its vicinity— a phenomenon known as allelopathy. In the wild, this toxicity stifles competition for water and nutrients, but it also limits the tree's value as a yard feature.

The world's largest walnut orchard is the 1,800-acre (730-ha) Shahmirzad orchard in Iran, although further east Kyrgyzstan has 550,000 acres (222,200 ha) of walnut forest, which is the remnants of a Central Asian subtropical forest from the Tertiary period.

BAOBAB

Adansonia spp.

The strange silhouette of the baobab with its squat trunk up to 100 feet (30 m) high and rootlike branches is instantly synonymous with African landscapes, but it also grows in parts of Australia. Its alternative name is "upside-down tree." According to one African tale, when the world was created every animal was given a tree to plant and the mischievous hyena thrust the baobab into the soil the wrong way up.

There are eight species of baobab: six from Madagascar, one native species on the African mainland, and another found in Australia. These trees are important to local people, providing lumber and shade while the leaves and fruit provide valuable food.

In fact, the distinctive shape is a response to their generally arid environment. The thick pinkish or copper trunk is a reservoir capable of holding huge volumes of liquid. Likewise, its branches are bare during the dry season because it sheds its leaves to minimize water loss. Baobabs produce large white flowers, which only open at night and so are pollinated by fruit bats as they drink the nectar. Later these will turn into fruit that can be 1 foot (30 cm) long.

Development agencies have begun to promote the baobab fruit as a means of diversifying peasant incomes in southern Africa. They point out it contains six times as much vitamin C as an orange, twice as much calcium as milk, and is rich in iron, potassium, and antioxidants.

Baobabs support the lives of countless organisms from insects to birds to bush babies to elephants. One hollow baobab near Derby in Western Australia was used as a prison for aboriginal convicts during the 1890s, while "The Big Baobab Pub" has been built inside what is thought to be world's largest living baobab. This 49-foot- (15-m-) diameter tree grows at Sunland Farm in Limpopo Province, South Africa, and some claim it is one of the world's oldest trees. Precise dating is impossible because baobab timber lacks growth rings, but carbon dated core samples suggest it could be over 6,000 years old.

The circumference of a Baobab's characteristically broad trunk can vary significantly between wet and dry seasons. The tree behaves much like a succulent, storing masses of water in its trunk.

AN ANNIVERSARY

Many people will want to mark life's momentous events more than just once. Marriages, births, and other important family occasions are often remembered year after year on the appropriate day.

In many cases this is by way of a traditional private ceremony between husband and wife. This may be simply an exchange of cards, gifts, a meal, or it may be the renewal of vows. Because a traditional gift associated with the fifth year wedding anniversary is wood, you may consider planting a tree with your spouse. Oak trees are regarded as a symbol of solidity, flaming red maples are known for representing passion, and flowering crab trees represent eternal love. Likewise, family members may choose to arrange an annual gathering to celebrate a propitious moment or a private tragedy. Whatever the occasion, it can be given extra meaning by being staged beneath a tree planted to mark the event.

Practicalities

If this is a family occasion that is to be repeated for years to come, the tree should be properly marked. Time erodes our memories and the youngest generation will need an explanation, so recording the details of the ceremony on a plaque is worth considering (*see page 11*). A short poem or couplet can also pithily capture the moment when the tree was planted.

INSPIRATION

According to the Greek historian Herodotus, the shrine
of Dodona was founded by a priestess from the temple
of Zeus in Thebes. Dodona was captured and enslaved
by the Phoenicians, who sold her to the people of
northern Greece. There she founded an oracle under
an oak tree to pass on divine wisdom. In time, other
trees sprang up to create a sacred grove. Visitors would
come and ask for advice and the priests would answer
by interpreting the rustling of the sacred leaves.

Choice of tree

You could, perhaps, take a
leaf from this book and plant
an oak to symbolize heavenly
support. If so, start by
considering a species that
currently grows well in your
locality because this will be
the one most likely to flourish.

Alternatively, you might
prefer to pick an exotic or
ornamental tree that will
stand out as a memorial to
an important private event.
Before making your decision,
do check on suitability for
your particular soil conditions
and climate first. Consider the
acidity, drainage, and soil type
of your chosen planting site.

Most important, pick
a healthy specimen suited
to the location. There is no
point in planting a delicate
tree, such as a lemon, in
areas that get several months
of snow cover each winter,
for example, and likewise
a small backyard will soon
be dwarfed by some of the
fast-growing conifers.

HOW TO USE TREES FOR FUEL

Extracting energy from wood was humankind's oldest and most important early technological breakthrough— far outweighing the oft-cited wheel. Fire allowed our ancestors to descend from the trees, drive game into traps, make inedible foods digestible, and heat shelters in chilly parts of Europe and North America.

Trees have been used for fuel for millennia.

Concerns over global warming are seeing wood coming back into favor. Burning wood is carbon-neutral because any gases released are those absorbed as the wood grew. Timber is also by far the most efficient means of converting solar energy into usable power. Better still, it stores this in a convenient natural battery.

However, there is more to harnessing the heat than simply applying a match. Open fires allow 90 percent of the heat to escape up the chimney, which wastes energy and reduces combustion temperatures. Using cast-iron and ceramic stoves can reduce waste to 20 percent by giving control over air intake, while waste gases are circulated to extract as much heat as possible. Modern furnaces that use wood pellets or chips instead of fossil fuels can be even more efficient and automated to minimize maintenance.

FUEL VALUE

Denser woods, such as hickory, oak, and beech, have the highest calorific value, and burn steadily but slowly. Dry softwoods, such as pine and spruce, burn hot, but fast. You can even out these variations by mixing up the lumbers.

Freshly cut lumber burns poorly because of its high water content. Moisture levels do vary between species and seasons, so a spring-felled cottonwood might contain 70 percent water while a winter-harvested walnut tree could have half this.

To burn well, the water content of wood should be below 25 percent. This is easily achieved by drying or "seasoning." Ideally fresh logs should be split to about 4 inches (10 cm) in diameter and stored off the ground under shelter with a good airflow. Spring-felled lumber generally needs at least two years' drying, but winter-cut trees might be used as fuel after a year. The wood is ready to burn when the bark comes away easily and the exposed grain is covered with small splits.

REDWOODS

Metasequoia, Sequoiadendron, Sequoia

The redwoods comprise three genera of living coniferous trees: Metasequoia glyptostroboides (*the dawn redwood*), Sequoiadendron giganteum (*the giant sequoia*) and Sequoia sempervirens (*the coast redwood*), *but the name "sequoia" is often used as a general term to include all of them. These three species, native to California and Oregon, include the "Titans"—the world's tallest trees.*

The largest giant sequoia, "General Sherman," at 275 feet (83 m), is not the tallest Titan, but with a volume of 52,510 cubic feet (1,487 m³) it is currently the world's largest tree. The largest living coast redwood is the "Lost Monarch," which is 320 feet (98 m) tall with a trunk measuring 26 feet (8 m) in diameter at breast height. Another coast redwood, "Hyperion," at 379 feet (116 m) is currently the world's tallest tree. Despite its immense stature, it was only discovered in 2006 growing in a gully in Redwood National Park.

The very tallest redwoods grow in deep mountain gullies, where they are protected from the worst weather and receive a plentiful water supply. Fossil evidence suggests that these trees perhaps formed the upper canopy of a temperate rainforest ranging over the whole Northern Hemisphere. The timber is highly

The sheer size of the trees means the
only feature most observers see in any detail
is the rusty soft bark of the huge trunks.

valued, being light, strong, and resistant to rot and fire. As a result, 96 percent of the natural redwood forests had been felled by the time logging ceased in 1978. Today's production comes from second-growth managed plantations, not only in California and Oregon, but also in south-eastern parts of the country and Hawaii, Mexico, New Zealand, and Europe.

OAK

Quercus robusta spp.

～

It would be fair to say that no tree has played a more important part in our history. Since the last ice age, members of this genus of slow-growing trees have underpinned almost every aspect of European and North American development.

The common pedunculate-fruited English oak.

There are approximately 400 members of the *Quercus* genus. Most are deciduous trees that have large diameter trunks and are capable of living for many centuries.

The most familiar oak trees are probably the deciduous trees of North America, Europe, and Asia. These have the familiar lobed leaves and produce acorns each fall.

Less well-known, however, are the 150-odd species of evergreen ring-cupped oaks from Southeast Asia.

Oak timber is extremely hard and strong. Until recently it was the lumber of choice for architects and builders. Up to the late nineteenth century almost all European and American ships were built from oak. It is still extensively used in flooring and furniture and the traditional technique of green-oak framing (making prefabricated buildings by pegging together unseasoned lumber) is enjoying a revival.

Oak is also in demand by the alcohol industry: the wood is high in tannins and vanillins and fine wine and spirits are stored in oak barrels to develop further dimensions of flavor and aroma as they mature. Stoppers made from the bark from the cork oak (*Q. suber*) seal out fungi and bacteria, yet are porous enough to allow the contents to age slowly. Oak smoke is useful in food processing, conveying subtle flavors to fish, meat, and cheese. The tannin-rich bark has been used for centuries by the tanning industry and in medicines.

ECOLOGICAL IMPORTANCE

The tree is vital for wildlife. Its dense foliage and rotting wood feeds innumerable insects, birds nest in its cavities, and the acorns fatten squirrels and larger mammals. It is capable of great age and size—some stalwarts may be many centuries old. Scientists estimate the average 200-year-old oak supports over 250 animal species.

FALL

~~~~~~~

Not for nothing did the first American settlers rename "autumn." Although color change in leaves occurs wherever deciduous trees are found, New England's spectacular tapestry of color at the end of summer as its woods shed their leaves is one of the natural wonders of the world.

The underlying chemistry associated with the change in color is inextricably tied in with photosynthesis—the process whereby green plants use sunlight to convert water and carbon dioxide into sugars. Photosynthesis, which literally means "putting together with light," relies on five distinctively colored chemicals. The two main ones, chlorophylls A and B, are green and continually produced as long as there is sufficient light. Their stronger color masks the presence of the lesser-known pigments, mainly orange carotene, and yellow xanthophyll. In late summer, shorter days and cooler nights mean that chlorophyll production drops off, but the carotene remains unaffected. This explains why healthy late-summer foliage pales and yellows.

Meanwhile, the tree prepares to shed its leaves by sealing them off at the base with a layer of corky cells. These slow the movement of sugars back to the trunk. As a result, carbohydrates concentrate in the leaf, particularly when the weather is sunny and dry. These react with proteins to

The shorter days and cooler temperatures of fall signal the tree to begin its "dormant" period, and shed its leaves.

produce anthocyanin, another vibrant pigment. The strong shades of red or purple in anthocyanin overpower the greens and yellows of the original leaf.

The vibrant colors hit their peak when chillier nights coincide with sunny daytime conditions—particularly when the preceding summer has been hot and dry. Because the chemicals of each tree species are different their leaves turn different colors: maples become scarlet, hickory becomes bronze, and birch turns gold. The multicolored effect is further enhanced when there is a mixture of deciduous species, interspersed with evergreens, growing on varied soil types. This brilliant combination is typical of New England— hence its world-famous fall—but is also mirrored around temperate zones in both hemispheres, especially East Asia, including China, Korea, and Japan.

A RETIREMENT

Leaving the workforce is one of the greatest changes in life. Many cultures recognize this by a tree to symbolize the passing of the baton from one office holder to another. In Canada, for example, it is customary for a retiring governor-general to join their successor in planting two trees to mark the passing of the baton.

NEW CHALLENGE

Most of us look forward to the moment when we stop work and can enjoy life at a slower pace. No longer will we be locked into a routine; instead we can relax and enjoy the good things in life. At least, that is the dream, but unfortunately, many of us rapidly find retirement boring. As a result, this is the perfect time to take on a new challenge and what better way than to plant an arbor, a tranquil place in which to relax with your life partner and watch the sun go down?

Inspiration

The idea has its roots in classical literature. In ancient Greece, poets and thinkers reveled in the notion of a *locus amoenus* ("pleasant place"), an idealized yard that included trees, grass, and water. This imaginary spot was usually set in a remote location and often highlighted the differences between urban and rural life, with suggestions of freedom or timeless immortality.

The archetypal leafy arbor is the Garden of Eden in the Bible, but the idea of a rural haven was also developed by the great Roman poets, Virgil and Horace. It crops up in medieval literature, too, and later was adopted by William Shakespeare. His lovers and fairies cavort through paradisiacal woodland in *A Midsummer Night's Dream,* while the setting for *As You Like It* is Shakespeare's local silvan idyll, the Forest of Arden.

Choice of tree

Clearly it is beyond most people's strength or pockets to plant a forest paradise. A small shady grove, on the other hand, is very achievable.

One speedy, but rewarding plan is to place a beautiful bench in a peaceful, secluded spot from which to consider the evening light.

A small clump of hazel provides shade, adorned with pretty catkins in spring and wildlife-attracting nuts in fall. Or a semicircular row of hornbeam facing southwest to catch the setting sun. These have thick, light green foliage in summer, yet in winter the now russet brown leaves cling to the branches to give shelter and privacy.

Or better still plant a mixed hedge, blending fruit and thorn, dark and light foliage to provide a wildlife haven and constant sources of interest and wonder.

HOW TO CLONE

Deciduous trees are remarkably vivacious. As well as rejuvenating from cut surfaces (see pages 42 and 52), many species are easy to "layer" and will root from cuttings. These qualities can be exploited to clone new stock—or even make a living yard feature.

To layer

- Trees, such as figs, are routinely propagated by scratching the bark of a tall branch that can be bent to ground level.
- In spring or summer, when the sap is running, peg the cut to the ground (ideally after brushing the damaged surface with hormone rooting powder).
- After about two months roots will have developed.
- Sever the parent limb and pot the rooted section.
- Grow in a greenhouse until large enough to transplant.

To air layer

- Repeat as above, but instead of pegging a branch to the ground, cut the base of a plastic bag and slip it over the scratched branch.
- Tie the bag tightly on one side of the cut and fill with a growing medium (sphagnum moss or a soil/sand mix).
- Water well and tie up the loose end. Check regularly to ensure the growing medium remains damp.
- Once the roots have developed, sever the branch and transplant.

To grow from cuttings

- Cut a 6-inch (15-cm) twig with a sharp knife, leaving one bud.
- Push into a damp, rich soil mix.
- Keep well watered.
- Plant outdoors when it is growing strongly.

Growing trees from cuttings has several benefits over other propagation methods, not least a mature tree in a shorter space of time.

TO MAKE A LIVING TREE HOUSE

1. Mark out a 5-foot (1.5-m) circle in early spring. Dig out a trench 6 inches (15 cm) deep and 6 inches (15 cm) wide around the circumference. Fill it with a soil mix and rake to produce a fine seed bed. Water heavily.

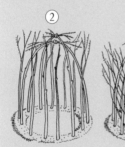

2. Push the thick ends of 7-foot (2-m) lengths of freshly cut willow osiers into the soil at 8-inch (20-cm) intervals.

3. Bend the free ends to the center and tie. Push shorter lengths of willow between the tallest osiers and weave in diagonally.

4. Keep weaving new growth into the structure. Remove excessive growth or stems growing in the wrong direction. In time, the structure will fill out.

Keep the soil moist and by midsummer you should have a living igloo. Clip regularly to keep its shape.

SPRUCE

Picea spp.

❧

The largest unbroken stretch of forest in the world, the taiga circles the Northern Hemisphere, passing through Alaska, Canada, Scandinavia, and Russia. The evergreen coniferous spruce is one of its dominant species, capable of withstanding fierce winds and temperatures of -40° F (-40° C).

There are some 35 *Picea* species, but the most familiar is probably the Norway spruce (*P. abies*) that forms the center piece of many Christmas displays. The conical canopy of dark green needles needs little introduction, but a closer examination shows that the needles grow in a spiral around the branches, shedding to leave a rough callous on the bark. In ideal conditions, they can grow up to 60–200 feet (20–60 m), although weather conditions are so harsh across much of its range 30–50 feet (10–15 m) is more usual.

*Norway spruce (*Picea abies*).*

Although a cold-climate specialist, the spruce is in effect a desert plant. The sub-Arctic may see plenty of rain and snow, but most of the year subzero temperatures mean that water is locked away. The tree's response is to have a sugary sap with antifreeze qualities while its needles are coated with a thick waxy coat that resists desiccation.

Despite these adaptations, the spruce grows well in milder climates, too. Huge regions of this cone-shaped tree are forested in temperate climates across the world. If allowed to mature, spruces can grow to 196 feet (60 m) tall, although most of this fast-growing crop is replanted as soon as it is harvested, making the spruce an infinitely sustainable source of lumber.

In the home, the spruce is probably most familiar as the Christmas tree. This practice of bringing a tree indoors and adorning it with seasonal decorations traces its history to Germany's pagan past, but it was spread across the English-speaking world by Queen Victoria's husband, Prince Albert of Saxe-Coburg, who allowed his family to be pictured standing next to one at Osborne House on the Isle of Wight in 1848.

There are many claimants to the title of the world's oldest tree, but genetically speaking a Scandinavian spruce, "Old Tjikko," beats them all at 9,600 years old. This "clonal" tree is growing in Sweden. The original has long-since died, but the root system lives on, throwing up suckers today.

FUNGI

In the minds of many, fungi are a sign of decay and death, but these primitive organisms, neither plant nor animal, are vital to trees. Over 60 species may be associated with a single veteran. Some are harmful, but most perform useful roles. Indeed, our forests could not exist without fungi.

Roots

A tree's roots are surrounded by a vast web of microscopic fungi that work ceaselessly to extract nutrients from the soil. Scientists may be able to use fungi as a way of removing pollution from the environment. Some simply break down leaf litter, but others scavenge for scarce nutrients, many of which are passed into the tree's roots in return for its sugars. Other species go further, attracting tiny invertebrates, only to trap and eat them—releasing nutrients to the host tree.

Trunk

Fresh wood is almost completely indigestible, so many forest creatures rely on fungi to start the process of breaking down the cellulose and lignin in the trunk. Woodworm beetle larvae are an exception—but even they rely on microscopic gut yeasts to cut up the long carbohydrate chains into digestible sugars.

Destruction

Some fungi are pure parasites and can kill a healthy tree, but others can actually prolong

Hollows may form from natural forces, including fungi growth.

its life by rotting the center of a heavy solid trunk to make a light strong cylinder that better resists gales. The newly created chamber becomes a home for birds, bats, and insects, which provide the tree with nutrients by way of their droppings and urine.

Bark

Over 100 species of lichen may colonize the surface of a single tree. These primitive organisms, half-fungi, half-algae, have plantlike abilities to manufacture sugars and to "fix" airborne nitrogen in soluble compounds, many of which can be absorbed by the tree.

Food

Finally, of course, forest fungi are highly prized by chefs for their unique flavor—truffles, porcini, chanterelles, shiitake, and oyster mushrooms are just some of the many edible species that can only grow underneath trees.

BRISTLECONE PINE

Pinus aristata, P. longaeva, P. balfouriana spp.

Bristlecone pines are widely accepted as the oldest single living organisms in existence. A few individuals are proven to be nearly 5,000 years old. These gnarled evergreens are found scattered across arid regions in six of the western states in North America, where they tolerate a harsh, exposed environment. As a result, the trees have very few competitors for the scarce resources on offer, and they are very resistant to infestation by pests and diseases.

There are three members of this group of pines: the Rocky Mountains bristlecone pine (*Pinus aristata*), which is found in Colorado, New Mexico, and Arizona; the Great Basin bristlecone pine (*P. longaeva*), found in Utah, Nevada, and California; and the foxtail pine (*P. balfouriana*), found in California. All are high-altitude specialists, and grow just above the tree line at about 6,560 feet (2,000 m) in the Rocky Mountains and High Plains.

Because of conditions high in the arid mountains, the trees grow slowly—the needles can last for 20, even 30 years, helping the bristle-cones to survive years of stress. Most of the tree's energy is devoted to survival, rather than size. The climate and the tree's great longevity also means it often outlives its own timber which is scoured smooth by wind, sand, and ice to leave a twisted trunk that is little more than a fragment of bark and wood.

The most ancient current specimen is nicknamed "Methuselah" and grows in the White Mountains of eastern California. Core samples taken in 1957 showed it to be 4,789 years old, but another bristlecone, "Prometheus," felled by researchers in 1964, had 4,844 growth rings, later revised to 4,862.

The trees' great age means their growth rings are of huge value to dendochronologists (*see page 78*). These scientists can use the cross section from a single tree to plot a continual time line back through several millennia. Stands of dead trees located even higher than today's living specimens suggest the local climate was milder at some point in the relatively recent past.

The pine's timber is very dense and this and its resinous sap strengthens its resistance to damage by insects, fungi, and other potential pests. The same cannot be said for souvenir hunters, and the U.S. Forest Service guards the location of the oldest trees to prevent vandalism.

Bristlecone pine cones are gray or dark brown and tipped with a slender, curved bristle.

IN MEMORIAM

The passing of a loved one is always painful. Whether unexpected or foreseen for many months, their sudden absence and the knowledge they will never return is often most difficult to accept.

Wakes and funerals are the formal rites by which we mark someone's passing— so too memorials in the form of shrines and tombstones. However, sometimes a living tribute is just as appropriate.

A growing tribute is surely the ultimate mark of respect. Unlike even the most beautiful of man-made monuments, it is a constant living testimony to the deceased.

Cremations require bereaved friends and relatives to find the most appropriate site for scattering the ashes. Often the deceased has left instructions or their passions and pastimes which make finding the perfect place easy. But where the choice is not clear, a tree can provide the answer.

All living things need the same chemical building blocks and the ashes are still full of minerals like carbon, and potassium. By planting a tree in an ash-lined pit, the physical essence of a person will be incorporated into the cells of a tree that will live on for many more decades, centuries, even millennia.

As the tree matures and changes, it will be admired for its beauty for years to come, benefiting not only the bereaved but also future generations who never knew the departed. As it grows it will also inspire the best of human emotions: happiness, energy, faith, devotion, and a love of beauty. In doing so, it carries forward the memory of the departed in a living, vital way that can only grow over the years. One day, it may even provide the lumber to make a treasured object.

Choice of tree

In warm climates, a ceiba (the Mayan tree of life) could be apt, while in cold regions species of yew, holly, or oak resonate with European cultures. Alternatively, search for a tree that matches the passions of the departed, be it walnut for the sportsman, magnolia for the fashion conscious, or olive for a cook. Or perhaps the departed left a childhood anecdote of happy days playing beneath a willow or whittling a hickory peg. The most important thing is that the living can connect to their loved one with a vibrant, growing memorial.

Inspiration

The Mayans believed in a world tree whose roots, trunk, and branches connected the underworld with the sky and the living. Similarly ancient European peoples revered the yew, holly, mistletoe, and ivy, plants that remained green and berried in the depths of winter when all else seemed dead. Later, Christians adapted these beliefs by planting yew trees in their churchyards and incorporating the shrubs into Christmas traditions. An evergreen is one way of showing that the love goes beyond the grave.

BALLED & BURLAPPED

Traditionally, you can buy and plant larger landscape trees "balled and burlapped," which means that growth has started and the root-ball is intact, wrapped in burlap. The best time to plant trees is in the fall, ideally, or in spring. Remember to keep the rootball watered.

• Measure the root-ball, and dig a sloping hole about three times as wide and a little deeper than the height of the root-ball. Water the hole well.

• Carefully lower the root-ball into the hole, burlap and all, so that the bottom of the trunk sits just above the soil surface. Cut away and remove any nonorganic wrapping, being careful not to damage the fragile roots. Gently tease out roots from the root-ball to encourage them to grow outward. Water in well.

• Replace the soil until the hole is halfway filled, and then tamp it lightly by gently stamping on the earth. Ensure the tree is standing upright, then water it slowly, saturating the soil. Finish off by filling in the rest of the soil.

• The soil should be kept moist for the first year after planting. If you spot wilting leaves, water immediately. Mulching above the roots with compost helps to retain moisture, but keep the mulch away from the trunk to prevent rotting.

HOW TO PLANT A BURLAPPED SAPLING

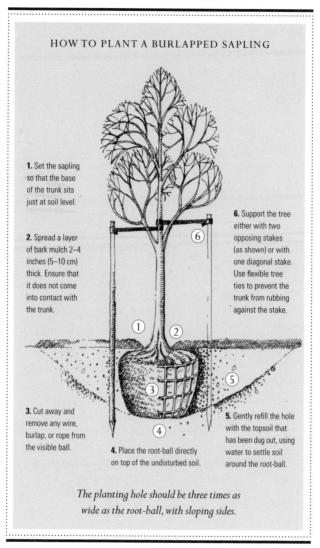

1. Set the sapling so that the base of the trunk sits just at soil level.

2. Spread a layer of bark mulch 2–4 inches (5–10 cm) thick. Ensure that it does not come into contact with the trunk.

6. Support the tree either with two opposing stakes (as shown) or with one diagonal stake. Use flexible tree ties to prevent the trunk from rubbing against the stake.

3. Cut away and remove any wire, burlap, or rope from the visible ball.

4. Place the root-ball directly on top of the undisturbed soil.

5. Gently refill the hole with the topsoil that has been dug out, using water to settle soil around the root-ball.

The planting hole should be three times as wide as the root-ball, with sloping sides.

YEW

Taxus spp.

This slow-growing, primeval forest tree is found around the Northern Hemisphere and into the Tropics. Although botanists split the world's yews into about nine species, the genetic distinctions are borderline.

Yew trees are long-lived, medium evergreen conifers, with reddish bark and dark green leaves arranged in two flat rows. Younger trees tend to sprout tall branches from a main trunk to produce a conical shape, while older trees can produce huge, sprawling specimens.

Berried or common yew.

The yew is capable of living for many centuries. Some of these ancient trees are still alive—the Fortingall Yew in Scotland is thought to be over 2,000 years old, and it is possibly the oldest living tree in Europe.

The yew was worshipped by pagans, and early Christians echoed this reverence by founding churches next to the trees. Most of the U.K.'s ancient yews are found in cemeteries.

The yellow/red timber of yew is not only beautiful, but highly prized; the outer yellow wood is very springy, whereas the red heartwood resists compression. This made it the perfect material for the longbow, which dominated European warfare until the sixteenth century. This demand for yew led to serious overharvesting of yews across continental Europe and numbers have yet to recover. Most of Europe's ancient yews are to be found in the U.K. because the timber there was inferior in quality.

In 1966, yew bark was discovered to contain powerful cancer-killing toxins named taxanes. Huge numbers of yews were harvested, particularly in North America and in India, provoking protests from environmental activists, including Al Gore.

Taxus baccata.

Fortunately the leaves of the common European yew tree (*T. baccata*) now provide a more renewable source of the drug.

Almost every part of the yew is toxic apart from the sweet red flesh (or aril) of the berries, which are an important source of winter food for birds; they swallow the berries and seed whole. Fortunately, although the seeds are highly toxic, it is covered with a hard indigestible coating, allowing it to pass harmlessly through the avian gut to germinate wherever it is deposited.

INDEX